LEARNING HOW TO SUCCEED

By John Taccarino, Ph.D.

With chapter contributions from
Dr. Mara Leonard, Dr. An Chi Cheng, Joseph Cheng,
Megan Ambrose, Meghan Huffman, John Leonard,
Rachel Bomher, Esther Velazquez and Sarah Royster

M⊙tivational PRESS®
LEADERS IN GLOBAL PUBLISHING

Published by Motivational Press, Inc.
1777 Aurora Road
Melbourne, Florida, 32935
www.MotivationalPress.com

Manufactured in the United States of America.

ISBN: 978-1-62865-435-6

CONTENTS

PART ONE

Applications of the S(Success)-Factor in Helping Students to Learn How to Succeed

PART 2

Case Study Insights into the Developmental and Educational Uses and Applications of the theory of the S-Factor

PART 3

Profiles of Individuals Who Have Used the Strengths of Their S-Factors to Achieve Greatness

PART 4

Morality, Ethics and the S-Factor

DEDICATION AND ACKNOWLEDGEMENTS

This book is dedicated to the memory of Dr. Mara Leonard whose ideas and spirit contributed so much to the concept of the S-Factor.

I further wish to sincerely thank my associates Leslie Wang, Javed Rahman, Nimod Athiyarath, Eva Chau and Jenny Sun at MirrorWalk, Ltd. for their highly significant contributions in developing and supporting S-Factor assessment and moving forward the applications of the S-Factor in the area of transformative personal development as expressed in this book.

Many thanks to David Ladon for his dedicated editorial efforts that helped move this manuscript to completion.

PART ONE

Applications of the S(Success)-Factor in Helping Students to Learn How to Succeed

CHAPTER 1

LEARNING HOW TO SUCCEED

By John Taccarino

Learning how to succeed is as important for students as learning how to read or write. There are essentially seven foundations for success that students have to learn and apply in order to be ready to succeed when they enter adult life and the world of work.

1. Choosing a career area that fits one's personality type
2. Choosing a career area that one is passionate about and gives meaning to one's life.
3. Choosing a career area where one has the aptitudes and talents that will give one the chance to succeed
4. Preparing oneself for success through education, training and developmental experiences
5. Studying and applying in one's own life the paths to success that have been followed by those who have succeeded at the highest levels
6. Becoming psychologically ready to succeed by developing a strong S(Success) Factor. This may involve committing

oneself to a process of S-Factor transformation through the use of habituated intention.

7. Learning how to succeed in morally and ethically appropriate ways

Perhaps the most important foundation for success is learning how to become psychologically ready to succeed by developing a strong S(Success). Factor. The **S (Success) Factor**, as presented in this book, is based upon an original theoretical construct developed by Dr. John Taccarino and Dr. Margaret Leonard. Dr. Taccarino and Dr. Leonard view the **S (Success) Factor as a global force within a person's structure of self which is formed and generated by the dynamics and interactions of the following core character and personality elements: internal motivation and self-regulation, self valuing, affective effectiveness, interpersonal effectiveness, self potency and success drive** (Taccarino, 2015). The S-Factor in many ways can be seen as an indicator of overall personality effectiveness in the areas of academic achievement and personal development. The S-Factor can be understood as varying in strength from individual to individual depending upon the relative stimulation, development and maturation of its interrelated elements that have been noted. The S-Factor in itself will not alter a person's inherited characteristics or talents, but a strong S-Factor can energize individuals to develop their abilities and help them to perform at the higher end of their potential. There is strong evidence, based upon a body of research findings (Appendix A) that the S-Factor is effective as an indicator of academic achievement, occupational performance, emotional intelligence, leadership potential, interpersonal effectiveness and personality effectiveness.

The present developmental patterns associated with the relative strength of a student's S- Factors can be obtained via the **Taccarino-Leonard S(Success)Factor Assessment - for Kindergarten/Young Children;** the **Taccarino-Leonard S(Success)Factor Assessment - for Primary Schools ;** and the **Taccarino-Leonard S(Success)Factor Assessment - for Middle-High Schools and Colleges.** These S-Factor assessments can be accessed on line at Mirrorwalk.com. in English and Future Education Group in Chinese language forms.

For young children and kindergarten students S-Factor assessment can help identify a child's early psychological readiness to achieve in school based upon the assessed strength or weakness of his/her emerging S-Factor and its interrelated elements. A child that displays weakness in the development of his/her S-Factor could be significantly aided by counseling and other interventions to prevent a pattern of underachievement in a child from becoming entrenched to the point it impedes future academic performance.

The **Taccarino-Leonard S(Success)Factor Assessment - for Kindergarten/Young Children** can be employed to monitor a student's S-Factor development and can be an early indicator of underachievement problems schools associated with a weak S-Factor. An analysis of the elements of s student's S-Factor profile can provide bases for identifying critical areas for S-Factor development and suggest avenues for assistance.

`The **Taccarino-Leonard S(Success) Factor Assessment** for **Primary School Students** can be employed to assess the

S-Factor development of students in the primary grades. For students who display S-Factor weakness in these grades it is crucial to put in place effective avenues for intervention and development.

The **Taccarino-Leonard S(Success)Factor Assessment - for Middle-High Schools and Colleges** can be employed in middle school, high school or college settings to help evaluate individuals for programs' that have high performance expectancies. It can also be valuable in high school or college counseling settings for assessing characteristics and tendencies which underlie psychological bases for under-achievement that go beyond variables such as study habits and external motivational factors. Via an analysis of responses to critical items, the counselor or educator can assist the student in targeting areas that may be focused upon to help him/her display more effective achievement patterns. S-Factor assessment can be seen as particularly useful when used to screen for underachievement and social adjustment problems among freshmen year students and to help identify the sources of underachievement and behavior problems.

In the area of career planning, S-Factor assessment can assist the individual to identify whether his present achievement tendencies fit the expectancies and demands of a given occupation and to isolate bases for change, which can help improve his/her success potential. It does not identify a person's aptitude for performance in a given area, but it does help to assess how effectively the individual will utilize his/her potential for performance Taccarino and Leonard's S-Factor construct has been developed with data-driven research as its foundation. The core of the theory is based upon a factor analysis of data obtained from research associated with the development of a broad based personality inventory. As has been previously indicated a number of research studies have been conducted by Taccarino and others (Appendix A) that support the validity of the theoretical construct of the S-Factor as it relates to its effect upon academic performance, personal effectiveness and career success. Further evidence relating to the S-Factor and the validity of the interrelated elements of the S-Factor as success readiness indicators can be found in Part 3 of this book. The pattern of research evidence strongly suggests that a dominant S-Factor is engine of success for those who have achieved at the highest levels.

S-FACTOR TRANSFORMATION IN HIGH SCHOOL AND COLLEGE STUDENTS

S-Factor development in young children is discussed later in this chapter, but S-Factor change in underachieving middle school, high school and college students should be seen more as a transformative process than a developmental process. A developmental process invites progress, but a transformation requires radical change. A middle school student or high school student with a weak S-Factor has already developed a pattern of poor S-Factor functioning that has become entrenched and embodied in his/her personality and perceptions. Many students who demonstrate patterns of academic underachievement despite high levels of potential have weak S-Factors and exhibit habit patterns that have caused them to see themselves and life in ways that are destructive of life success and academic achievement

To understand the bases of S-Factor transformation we have to look at it the way Aristotle viewed the acquisition of virtue. Aristotle contended that the most important factor in the effort to achieve happiness is the development of good moral character. To Aristotle virtue is not a passive state, but is something that is built by repeated actions until a virtue becomes part of a person's character. In other words, the individual needs to develop the habit of being virtuous to become a virtuous person. Essentially the habit of being virtuous becomes part of who one is as a person. Essentially habits are the traits and characteristics of your personality that define who you are and how you see and react to life. Habits develop through repeated action. We can observe this process in the movie Groundhog Day, in which Bill Murray's character, Phil, experiences a time loop – reliving February 2 over and over again. At the film's start, Phil is misanthropic and curmudgeonly. However, as he experienced the same day on repeat, he began a process of personal transformation, seeking to improve his behavior each day. Through the repetition of virtuous behavior, Phil developed habits of virtue, and thus became a virtuous person.

This pattern can also be applied to the process of transforming a person with a weak S-Factor into a person with a strong S-Factor. The core S-Factor traits of self- valuing, internal motivation and self-regulation, affective effectiveness, self- potency and success drive are the virtues of the S-Factor. These success virtues can be achieved via the same process used when discussing character development. I call this process **habituated intention** when applied to the strengthening of the S-Factor and its key elements. To acquire the full operation of the S-Factor dynamics and its elements it is necessary for the person to manifest a high level of intent as a basis for change and transformation. . If a student is weak in any or all of the key elements of his /her S-Factor , what is required for S-Factor transformation is a conscious commitment to change whereby he/she visualizes how a person, for example, would exhibit self-potency in a life situation and then intentionally behave in that way. By repeatedly behaving in the way a person with strong self-potency would behave, such identifying and acting upon opportunities. Another example would be intentionally seeking to act in a manner consistent with how a person who was self-regulated would behave, such as staying on task despite distractions. In these examples, the more consistently the student would intentionally seek to display self potency and self-regulation in his/her behavior, the more likely he/she would begin to develop habits associated with this mode of behavior. The process of S-Factor transformation via **habituated intention** becomes more constant and persistent as the habits that build S-Factor strength become part of who the student is becoming and wants to become..

S-FACTOR DEVELOPMENT IN CHILDREN

A strong S-Factor can help a student to develop the psychological readiness that supports the processes of learning how to read and write as well as helping him/her to become psychologically prepared to achieve overall academic success at the highest levels of his/her potential. S–Factor development in children is a learning task that can be achieved through the process of **habituated intention** in much the same way a person's S-Factor can be transformed during adolescence and young adulthood. The difference, however, is that the bad habits of a weak S-Factor will not have to be overcome at the same level when seeking to develop strong S-Factors in young children. *Habituated intention* can be used to help children to form positive patterns of behavior that will provide a strong basis for academic, career and life achievement. Applying *habituated intention* in early childhood can build strong factor traits that will not require S-Factor transformation later in life.

The first step in developing strong S-Factors in children is to help them to develop an awareness of the importance of self-valuing, internal motivation and self-regulation, affective effectiveness, interpersonal effectiveness, self-potency and success drive as traits they need to manifest as foundations for their academic, career and life success. A significant amount of time and effort needs to be committed at home and in school to convince young children of the importance of reading and writing as a foundation for learning and achievement. As parents and educators, we must further emphasize that developing the traits of a strong S-Factor are just as necessary as reading and writing as foundations for their academic achievement and ultimately career success. Positive S-Factor development requires that children develop a conscious need to develop the psychological roots of success as manifested in the theory of the S-Factor. From an early age and forward, children need to be consistently encouraged to intentionally seek to develop the strong S-Factor habits of self-valuing , internal motivation and self-regulation, affective effectiveness interpersonal effectiveness, self-potency and success drive in order to provide the psychological bases for educational success A key way of convincing children that developing a strong S-Factors is important for them is to use stories and case studies of people such as Jack Ma and Oprah to help them to see how very successful people have used the habits of their strong S-Factors to support success attainment at the highest levels. Obviously there are forms of success that children can emulate that are not just based upon fame or wealth, but in the works of those such as Mother Theresa who achieved great life success in caring for those in great need. It is important to identify role models such as teachers and nurses who have cross- cultural relevance and have found ways to contribute and succeed in forms that provide great service to their communities and provide significant life meaning for these individuals. In specific course in school it can be demonstrated how a scientist such as Madame Curie used her strong levels of self- valuing, internal motivation and self-regulation to overcome gender bias in the scientific establishment to discover and apply the uses and applications of radium.

It is very important for the goals of S-Factor development in children to become imbedded in the goals of parents, school curriculums and course content. For example, it can be pointed out to children how historical figures in their countries and cultures used their strong S-Factors to succeed and achieve. In courses dealing with children's literature, for example, the strong S-Factors that may be found in some fictional characters can be emphasized and interpreted as bases for their success.

Just as we evaluate a student's educational progress in school via report cards, we need to evaluate a child's progress in developing S-Factor strength. When the student is made accountable for displaying positive S-Factor development the intent to develop strong S-Factors will be instilled early on as developmental goals as important as learning how to read and write.

THE CORE ELEMENTS OF THE
S-FACTOR

The following is a discussion of the core, interrelated elements of the S-Factor and their implications for building strong S-Factors and success readiness in students.

Internal Motivation and Self-Regulation

Is the student motivated from within? Is the student a self-starter? Does he/she have an internal locus of control that is expressed in self-discipline and self-regulation? Individuals who are internally motivated have a core structure of values that permit them to define life meaning and goals without the need for significant external direction or models. They are able to persist in task accomplishment without specific or immediate external rewards or punishments. Individuals who are internally motivated have a self-defined worldview that provides a strong basis for self-actualization and personal becoming. High achievers have personally significant life goals and act upon those goals.

Internal motivation is not being built effectively when the internal interests and goals of the child are made secondary to the interests and goals of curriculum consultants and test makers. Rather, curriculum goals should emerge from the interests of the student. I recall that as a seven-year old I was a horrible reader, tenth percentile in reading speed and comprehension. I dreaded being called upon to read aloud in class as much as I feared going to the dentist. Rather than sending me to a tutor or a summer session of remedial classes, my parents bought me annual subscription to the Sporting News as they knew I had a great love for the sport of baseball.. As soon as the Sporting News arrived each week, I voraciously read it cover to cover. The next time a reading test was administered to me in school, I scored at the 95th percentile. Not only did the Sporting News improve my reading, it stimulated an interest in the statistics of baseball. I now teach statistics in a university setting. From my own experiences and what I have observed in numerous students, it truly is interest driven internal motivation that builds a genuine and sustainable desire to learn and achieve

Internal motivation and self-regulation are interchangeable. Internal motivation leads to self-regulation. If the student is motivated internally rather than externally, he/she will be much more able and willing to self-regulate impulses and distractions that could block goal attainment. Persistence and resilience, key components of achievement, are primarily the products of internal motivation and self-regulation.

Developmental counseling can help the student to clarify and act upon his/her interests and form internally motivated goals. Understanding and using one's internal motivational structure is in many ways the essence of personal discovery and the roots of self-regulation and productive self-directed achievement. To achieve, the student first has to know what it is he/she really wants to achieve and then be able to persist in the process of goal attainment.

Self-Valuing

Does the student feel worthy of love, respect and success? Does the student value his/her life, accomplishments and goals?

Does the individual experience self-love in a significant way? Self-valuing permits the individual to be resilient in dealing with failure and persistent in seeking to accomplish what the student feels truly worthy of achieving. To compete and interact socially with others in effective ways, requires a strong core of self-valuing.

Too often the consequences of peer bullying, an impersonal learning environment and external pressures to perform on personally irrelevant tests tends to diminish and erode the student's value of self. Helping the student to achieve a foundation of love and respect for self should be perhaps the primary goal of developmental guidance. The student needs a foundation of self-love before he/she is ready to compete academically on a basis other than fear. Basic love of self is as or more important than an early mastery of basic skills as a preparation for success both in school and in the workplace.

Affective Effectiveness

Is the student able to regulate and use his/her affective self effectively? Emotions can be effective achievement motivators, but a student has to learn how to focus and use his/her emotions effectively. Emotional learning for the individual certainly is as or perhaps even more important than academic learning in preparing students for their present and future lives.

Is the student sensitive to and able to read the emotions of others? The ability to empathize and respond appropriately to emotional needs is very important in areas where the individual has to work with and motivate others in order to become successful in goal accomplishment.

Creativity and divergent thinking are also associated with affective effectiveness. The very nature of creativity has an affective, intuitive element that must be prized in students. The valuing and respect for creativity and divergent thinking are important elements in building strong S-Factors. Unfortunately the emphasis on developing convergent thinking and the passive role students are often asked to assume in large group learning experiences has traditionally made schooling less than an optimal environment for igniting imagination and creativity. Schooling too often delays the development and maturation of creativity in its students rather than sparking it. If school based experiences were more productive in spawning creativity in students we might see more cases where a young Ms. Moses impresses us with the creativity of her art, rather than have us wait until she becomes Grandma Moses. The chapter in this book that profiles Steve Jobs certainly draws attention to the failure of many schools to respond to the needs of creative, divergent thinkers like Mr. Jobs.

Affective effectiveness involves a type of emotional maturity that is the foundation for impulse control, resilience, social adaptability, self-governance and the ability to generate an enthusiasm for achieving goals both for oneself and others. The building or further development of a school's affective curriculum is an essential component in seeking to help students develop strong S-Factors.

Interpersonal Effectiveness

Is the student persuasive and able to effectively communicate his/her ideas to others? Does the student enjoy social interactions and does he/she appear well liked by his/her peers? Does the student appear self-assured and poised in social interactions? A person may have great ideas or a wonderful product to sell, but unless the individual can communicate the value of the idea or product to others in a socially effective way, success can always be just beyond the horizon. Interpersonal effectiveness is an essential component of the S-Factor that needs to be supported and developed at an early age.

Self-valuing, affective effectiveness and interpersonal effectiveness are heavily interrelated within the S-Factor. A proactive developmental guidance program should address the need for and the nature of novel school programs that help students to develop synergistic, interactive strengths within these three key components of the S-Factor.

Self-Potency

An individual's self-potency involves the level of energy, spontaneity, hope, joy of life, ambition, and excitement that the child brings to work and social interactions. It is associated with the student's internal motivational level and scope of interests, but it also speaks to the person's ability to project a powerful, energetic personality. Self-potency could connote terms like charismatic and larger than life, but may also apply to quieter and more subtle manifestations such as inner confidence, pervasive goodness, soul, quality of character, spirituality and courage

Students need help from parents, teachers and counselors to learn how to energize and project their personalities in positive rather than negative ways. They also need to be encouraged to act upon life rather than just reacting to their circumstances. As an example, I was once watching a group of young children leave the shore and run into the ocean on a day where the waves were high and hard breaking. The children were rushing directly into the waves, but were constantly being knocked back toward the shore. Eventually all the children returned to the beach except for one little girl who continued to try. Frustrated with her failure to reach the calm water beyond the waves, the girl was about to return dejectedly to the beach, but her parent encouraged her to act upon the wave, not just react to it by allowing herself to experience the wave's full force. A smile came to the girl's face as she looked at a new wave, which was one of the highest of the day, and began to run toward it. As the wave approached her, she dove under it and surfaced in the calm water beyond the waves. The girl was well on her way toward developing a strong sense of self-potency and a powerful personal dynamic.

Success Drive

Does the student have a strong work ethic? Does he/she persist, or even work harder, when failures mount? A yes to these questions is indicative of students with strong success drives. They are ambitious, self-motivated, resilient and have a strong need to succeed.

Children often exhibit a strong success drive early in life, but it has to be nurtured and encouraged to flourish. Children are excited by new experiences and want desperately to learn and succeed. Schooling, on the other hand, often frustrates a student's emerging success drive by emphasizing test important right answers in the context of instruction, providing passive, lecture based learning activities, and allowing the student to experience premature peer competition and put downs. Encouraging and valuing effort, regardless of the immediate outcome is essential in developing success drive. It is the ability to tolerate failure and to keep trying which is the basis for a sustainable work ethic and a powerful S-Factor. Long term accomplishments and progress in developing strong success tendencies ought to be the key assessment criteria in the schooling experience rather than the immediate, prematurely competitive, accounting defined by standardized achievement tests. In the storied race between the turtle and the hare, the hare certainly succeeded early and may very have done better than the turtle on the **Iowa Test of Basic Skills**, but the turtle's work ethic and strong success drive prevailed in the longer race

As previously noted, most children come to school with a strong desire to achieve, but by the time many reach the third grade their intrinsic motivation and sense of self value have been eroded by what they encounter in the schooling experience. A major challenge for a developmental guidance program is to define ways of sustaining and building upon the self-value and success drive most children bring with them when they enter the school's door with new pencils and new hopes. Hope and self-valuing are the engines of the success drive. Self-deprecation and discouragement are its flat tires. Unless we can build upon an early schooling experience that nurtures a student's success drive we will continue spending much of our time in the upper grades rebuilding students' sense of hope and self-worth.

REFERENCES

Taccarino, J., (2015). The Taccarino-Leonard S(Success)-Factor: *The Psychological Roots of Success.*, Melbourne, Florida: *Motivational Press*

CHAPTER 2

EFFECTIVELY USING OUR SCHOOLS TO HELP STUDENTS TO LEARN HOW TO SUCCEED

By John Taccarino

Is your school effectively helping its students to learn how to succeed? Are your school's teachers and students ready to succeed at the higher ends of their potentials? If your answers to both of these questions are yes, there is no need to read any further. On the other hand, if you wish to improve your school's culture for developing success readiness and building S-Factor strength among your students, this book could be of significant value to you and your school

Many schools teach for the test when they should be teaching for success. A school needs create the developmental bases for strong S-Factors and success readiness in its students. The first stage in the process of success readiness transformation should focus upon faculty development. Screening practices should be put in place to insure that candidates for new teaching positions exhibit strong S=Factors. An ongoing intervention program should be introduced to assist present faculty to strengthen their own S= Factors. When faculty members clearly manifest strong S-Factors themselves, they will be in a position to model and effectively develop success readiness in students.

To develop a school culture that supports and values S-Factor strength, it is important to immediately put in place a specific plan of action for S-Factor development and, if necessary, transformation. First, by defining a priority emphasis on the strengthening of each student's S-Factor, it can help redefine the schooling experience as something that should focus more upon preparing the individual to succeed and less upon the significance of the bean counting, competitive aspects of standardized testing.

Second, by assessing the present strength of a student's S-Factor, a personal success development plan can be formulated and implemented when intervention is defined as important. Third, if S-Factor formation is to become a focused goal of schooling, the relative strength of each student's level of S-Factor strength should be consistently monitored. By reporting the progress of a student's S-Factor development to his/her parents, it can help define success readiness maturation as a priority in the home as well as the school.

S-Factor assessment can be useful in lower grades, middle school, high school and counseling settings for evaluating characteristics and tendencies beyond variables such as study habits and external motivational factors that underlie the psychological bases for underachievement. In such applications, it can provide the diagnostic baseline for evaluating the present strength of an individual's S-Factor and help establish goals for developmental improvement or, if necessary, S-Factor transformation among long term underachievers.

An effective plan for developing a school's culture of success readiness has many facets, but a common goal. That goal asks each teacher and each student to make personal commitments to their own unique form of success and support the success potentials of others. To help their students to learn how to succeed, a given school must respond to the developmental needs of students at each stage of S-Factor development. Based upon S-Factor assessment: the following represents the needs of students at each level of S-Factor development:

S-FACTOR SCALE

Very Strong S-Factor

Students who score in this range tend to maximize their potential and are generally capable of displaying a consistent, persistent and focused levels of effort in their academic work despite obstacles and, or failures. They tend to be resilient and self-directed achievers who are well prepared on a personal level to compete and succeed in demanding academic programs. Much can generally be expected of them both in school and in their future careers. They also tend to be responsible and show leadership traits. If a student who scores in this range is in high school and has low or marginal SAT or ACT scores, but good grades, the compensating power of a very strong S-Factor could and perhaps should be used as an important criteria to support a positive decision for college admission.

Strong S-Factor

Students scoring in this range generally exhibit the tendency to be motivated, self-directed achievers who could perform well in most academic settings. They may also have leadership traits that show promise and can be further developed. Further strengthening their S-Factors could help prepare them to reach the highest peak of their potentials and improve their readiness to perform even more effectively in demanding academic programs or career settings. If a student who scores in this range is in high school and has low or marginal SAT or ACT scores, but good grades, the compensating power of a strong S-Factor could and perhaps should be used as a significant criteria to support a positive decision for college admission.

Moderately Strong S-Factor

Those scoring in this range are generally seen as having many positive tendencies that support an effective level of achievement. They normally could be expected to perform well in a supportive environment where they are given external direction, attainable rewards and are not faced with failure, serious personal problems or significant obstacles to their success. Their performance could, however, become less effective and focused if the work is very difficult, they become frustrated in attaining rewards, have serious personal problems or experience some level of perceived failure. Unless an individual who scores in this range can strengthen his/her S-Factor, he/she could possibly experience some difficulty in very challenging, stressful and competitive educational or career settings. Enhancing self-confidence, resilience and persistence should be key points of focus in helping them to strengthen their S-Factors. Fortunately they often have many S-Factor positives that can be built upon to stimulate a fairly rapid and effective development process if their personal motivation for change can be ignited.

Emerging S-Factor

Students who score in this range can generally be seen as on the bubble with respect to their S-Factors. They typically have some elements of emerging S-Factor strength, but they may also have problems in the areas of initiative, self-direction, persistence and resilience. They may not have the entrenched underachievement patterns associated with a very weak S-Factor, but are often seen as failing to achieve at their full potential. To prepare themselves for advanced education or immediate career goals, they need to urgently begin a process of S-Factor development or transformation. Fortunately they often have emerging S-Factor positives that can be built upon to stimulate a fairly rapid and effective development process if their personal motivation for change can be ignited.

Moderately Weak S-Factor

Persons scoring in this range have moderately weak S-Factors. They generally tend to require personally satisfying, immediate rewards to maintain effort. They can often be seen as having difficulty working independently and requiring a significant level of external direction and supervision in order to perform. They would tend to perform best on highly structured tasks. They may have some tendencies towards persistent underachievement that need to be addressed in counseling and other developmental programs. To prepare themselves for either advanced educational programs or immediate career goals, they need to urgently begin a process of S-Factor development or transformation. They generally have some existing positives that could be built upon, but they typically will need a great deal of help and encouragement to commit themselves to a process of success factor transformation. The first step involves helping them to realize that they may have a great resource of untapped potential for achievement that could be harnessed if they can begin to take ownership of that potential and act upon it.

Weak S-Factor

Individuals scoring in this range often have marked tendencies towards underachievement and could exhibit difficulties in the areas of impulse control and socialization. Emphasis should be placed on helping them to set realistic goals, maintain the consistency of their efforts and build their belief in their ability to succeed. They may require significant levels of supervision, support and encouragement to overcome what are possibly deeply entrenched tendencies that have limited the actualization of their potentials and made them doubtful of their ability to succeed. Certain individuals who score in this range may have experienced some level of academic success, but if that is the case, it is often due to superior aptitude. Although their intelligence and talent may allow them to marginally compete, their performance, however, may still be far below what they could be capable of achieving if they could work toward realistic goals, persist in their efforts despite obstacles and genuinely believe in their own worth. In many cases such individuals urgently need a wake-up call to face the reality of the success traits they will need to exhibit when the competition becomes stiffer in future academic or career settings.

Very Weak S-Factor

Individuals who score in this range are normally deeply entrenched underachievers who may also have difficulties in the areas of impulse control and socialization. They will generally require long term intervention. They are discouraged and, or have distorted views of their abilities and potentials for success. Their view of themselves, competition and the world generally has to be specifically redefined in order to provide a basis for meaningful change. Often they will blame others, luck or circumstances for their lack of achievement. They will commonly refuse to take personal responsibility for their failures. They have to first recognize that they have a problem that is within who they are and not outside themselves. They have to want to change and be willing to make the commitment to change. They also have to believe that their personal tendencies and perceptions can be changed. In many cases individuals who score in this category are passive victims who do not trust their capacities to change who they are and the circumstances in their environment. They need to be helped to believe in their ability to change and have a positive impact upon the world around them. By doing so, they can begin to redefine who they are and what they sincerely want to achieve in their lives.

S-Factor Profile

Scores derived from the subscales of the assessment represent the core S-Factor elements (self-valuing; internal motivation and self-regulation; affective effectiveness, interpersonal effectiveness; self-potency and success drive) are presented as the S-Factor Profile for each student. The profile displays areas of S-Factor strength and weakness that are specific to each core element. The S-Factor Profile can be used as a diagnostic tool for developing a plan of action for S-Factor development or transformation for each student.

PERSONALITY BASED PERFORMANCE STYLES

The **Taccarino-L eonard S(Success)Factor Assessment - for Kindergarten/Young Children, the Taccarino-L eonard S(Success)Factor Assessment - for Primary Schools and the Taccarino-L eonard S(Success)Factor Assessment - for Middle-High Schools and Colleges** are also effective in identifying personality based behavior styles that help define the student's present achievement tendencies via the following assessment scales: *Introversion/ extroversion Scale* and the *Creative/Analytical Scale.* Having a sense of the student's overall preferred style of behavior could assist the counselor in accommodating the process of S-Factor strengthening within the context of each student's preferred style of performance.

The Introversion/ Extroversion Scale

It is important for students to have an understanding of how their personality based behavior and learning styles interact with their level of S-Factor strength or weakness. Students typically have tendencies toward introversion or extroversion with the strength of these tendencies having important implications for academic, career and life choices. Ambiverts are those who have a mixture of introversion and extroversion tendencies, but they typically lean toward either introversion or extroversion.

Introverts tend to focus more upon their internal life and mental activities. They enjoy being alone or interacting with trusted friends and associates. Introverts like to think, read, use computers, watch , analyze and enjoy a quiet , reflective life. They seldom feel bored when they are alone and are more excited by ideas than social activities involving large groups. Inventors, composers, writers, artists and scientists are often introverts. Introverts may not be shy, but they just enjoy their private lives and trusted, intimate friends.

Extroverts, on the other hand, like to live outside themselves and prefer doing things more than observing things or reflecting on what they see or hear. They like to be around people, often large crowds of people, and commonly feel bored and unhappy when they are alone. They tend to be energized by people. They like to do things and see things in the company of others. They tend to be simulated by interacting with people and enjoy large parties, sports events and community gatherings. They tend to enjoy the social part of school more than the academic part. They are great joiners and love to be the center of attention. Because they are people persons, they like careers that involve working with people. Extroverts are often teachers, sales professionals, managers or political leaders.

Ambiverts, whether they have leanings toward introversion or extroversion may often be better able to adapt to school, career or life activities that are in opposition to the preferences of either extroverts or introverts. For example, a true introvert may have difficulty selling his/her idea to a group of people, while an ambivert with some introversion tendencies may be more able to adapt to what is needed in that situation.

The following are the personality based behavior styles that can be identified via S-Factor assessment:

Highly Introverted

Students whose scores fall in this range are seen as highly introverted and prefer solitary activities. They will tend to do well in performing analytical tasks and be capable of functioning independently without a great deal of external reinforcement. They either have or could be disposed to easily develop the important S-Factor element, **Internal Motivation and Self-Regulation**. They may, however, be challenged to adapt their personality patterns and preferences if they find themselves involved in activities or pursuits that require large group activities and interactions. They are capable of displaying or developing the S-Factor elements **Self-Valuing, Affective Effectiveness, Interpersonal Effectiveness, Self-potency** and **Success Drive,** but they tend to manifest these traits in more analytical, indirect and reflective ways than exroverts.

Introverted

Students whose scores fall in this range tend to like solitary activities and quiet time, but they can enjoy participating in small groups with other introverts who they like and trust. Although they are not as uncomfortable in large groups as extreme introverts, they prefer activities that value reflection, observation and analysis. They tend to take a while to warm up to people, but they can be an excellent friend if they find someone they like and trust.

They either have or could be disposed to develop the important S-Factor element, **Internal Motivation and Self-Regulation.** They may, however, be challenged to adapt their personality patterns and preferences if they find themselves involved in activities or pursuits that require large group activities and interactions. They are capable of displaying or developing the S-Factor elements **Self-Valuing, Affective Effectiveness, Interpersonal Effectiveness, Self-potency** and **Success Drive,** but they tend to manifest these traits in more analytical, indirect and reflective ways than extroverts. Also being introverted, does not mean they cannot be amusing or effective in social situations, they just prefer more intimate relationships and quieter times than extroverts.

Somewhat Introverted

Students who fall in this range are ambiverts who lean more toward introversion than extroversion. They can use their moderate introversion tendencies to check the possible impulsiveness of their extroversion and employ reflection and observation to help them to read social situations and the motives of others. They can be gregarious or reflective depending upon the mood, needs and nature of the situation. Individuals in this range can be both creative and analytical thinkers.

Somewhat Extroverted

Students who fall in this range are ambiverts who lean more toward extroversion than introversion. They can use their moderate extroversion to blend their analytical and reflective tendencies with spontaneity and a desire for social interaction. Individuals in this range can be both creative and analytical thinkers.

Extroverted

Students who are extroverts tend to be social, gregarious and outward rather than inward in their approach to life. Rather than reflecting and thinking, they prefer activities that involve spontaneity and action. They prefer working or having fun in groups and tend to be bored when they are alone. They often have or are able to develop key S-Factor traits such as **Self – Valuing, Affective Effectiveness, Self-Potency** and **Success Drive.** They can develop **Internal Motivation and Self-Regulation**, but they often have to go against their basic personality type and tendencies to do so.

Highly extroverted

Students who are highly extroverted tend to be very social, gregarious and outward rather than inward in their approach to life. Rather than reflecting and thinking, they clearly prefer activities that involve spontaneity and action.They prefer working or having fun in large groups and tend to be very bored when they are alone. They often have or are easily able to develop key S-Factor traits such as **Self –Valuing, Affective Effectiveness, Self -Potency** and **Success Drive.** They may, however, have difficulty developing **Internal Motivation and Self-Regulation** and to do so they will have to go against their basic personality type and tendencies in order to achieve some goal associated with their need for success.

THE ANALYTICAL/ CREATIVITY SCALE

The basic difference between students who are primarily analytical and those who are primarily creative is that they use different ways of learning and solving problems. Students with analytical personalities tend to do well in school because they seek to learn and solve problems through the application of reason and logic. They tend to be convergent thinkers. Schools tend to value and support convergent thinkers. On the other hand, students with creative personalities often do not do well in school because the way they think and learn is often out of synch with convergent thinking and formal logic. Creative students tend to be divergent thinkers. They think outside the box and are often rebellious when they are asked to think and learn in a school curriculum that is geared toward producing convergent thinkers. The Analytical /Creative Scale seeks to assess a student's relative place on the continuum between being very analytical or very creative. On the other hand, there are some students who are neither primarily analytical nor primarily creative who can manifest both analytical and creative tendencies within the structure of their personality. This scale can identify those students as well.

CHAPTER 3

COMBINING THE S-FACTOR AND FRANKL'S THEORY OF LOGOTHERAPY IN HELPING TO LEARN HOW TO SUCEED

By Kurtis Simonich

The theory of the S-Factor can be combined with other frameworks such as Frankl's theory of Logotherapy to assist students in learning how to succeed. Kurtis Simonich, a graduate of the Clinical Mental Health Counseling Program in the College of Education at DePaul University addresses bases for combining the theory of the S-Factor with Frankl's theory of Logotherapy to provide a broader foundation for assisting individuals to achieve significant change in their psychological readiness to achieve in school and succeed in life. This chapter is adapted from Mr. Simonich's contribution to the book " S (Success) Factor, the Psychological Roots of Roots of Success." (Taccarino et al, 2015)

The S-factor theory is within itself an intriguing concept because it draws together many previously conceived ideas, while converging with ideas that have not been explored as much in the literature. Before getting into details of what the S-Factor Theory is and how it can be applied in the context of a counseling strategy, it is important to establish the initial thoughts of why this theory should be paired with Logotherapy. First off, the S-Factor theory is built off of five major components that coincide with some of the central tenants of Logotherapy; thus providing a more thorough explanation of Frankl's developmental perspectives. Secondly, a man like Viktor Frankl can be considered an outlier when compared to members of the general society in regards to how he responded to so many adverse and traumatic incidents throughout his lifespan. Therefore, an in depth application of alternative theories such as the S-Factor seems necessary to make sense of such an intriguing man like Frankl. Also, the S-Factor theory does an appropriate job of describing what or how to reach a certain level of success; but it does not account for what will be described in this paper as *meaningful success*. This addition of *meaningful success* is exactly where Frankl's Logotherapy becomes a necessary and pertinent aspect in further developing the S-Factor theory. Also, Frankl's dedication to hope is a concept that is applicable and not limited to the helping profession; and in this case very present in the S-Factor Theory. Once this is accomplished, this dual-theory can be applied in both school counseling and explaining lifespan development in an advantageous manner.

VIKTOR FRANKL

In the year 1926, the inception of Logotherapy/Existential Analysis was introduced during a lecture to the Academic

Society for Medical Psychology. Viktor Frankl developed this idea of Logotherapy, only conceptually and without a name for it yet, through his experience in a few different arenas such as: Steinhoff Psychiatric Clinic, Viennese Mental Hospitals and Youth Counseling Centers (Batthyany 2010). At the time, Frankl was a part of the Individual Psychology Union learning the pathologies, typologies and therapeutic techniques of Individual Psychology. In that same lecture, Viktor defined his own largest concern being, "the formation of a therapeutic and theoretic program that should complement an understanding of neuroses based upon Alfred Adler's Individual Psychology (Frankl 1967). Frankl's concern was in the fact that an effective therapist must approach the client's outlook on therapy and the client's own life; not on the neuroses of the individual. During his time there, he became well acquainted with the heads of the Anthropological wing of the Physiological Institute of the University of Vienna, Oswald Schwartz and Rudolph Allers. Due to the philosophical and obviously anthropological nature of these two gentlemen, Frankl began to develop somewhat of his own perspective on the theory of Individual Psychology. While recognizing that the success of the therapeutic course depended entirely on the willingness and insight of the patient, Frankl believed there was more to this explanation. His twist on the course of therapy was attempting to understand the reason for the differences in client's motivation as an expression of an orientation towards life, and view them as relatively independent from the presenting problem (Batthyany 2010). Prior to this lecture proclaiming the faults of Individual Psychology, in 1925 Frankl stated,

"Neurotic patients cannot be happy because they have not grown into life, because they despise it, devalue it, and hate it. It is the task of the psychotherapist to fully give back the patients' love for life and will to community, and while not as empirical proofs, the therapist can easily re-instill these in the course of critical discussion of the value of living" (Frankl 1925).

This quote entirely sets the tone and creates a platform to understand the theoretical lens and overt outlook Frankl dedicated his life towards pursuing. Following this culmination of ideas, Frankl's decision to publicize his opinion on what could be considered one of the most influential theories of Psychotherapy, Rudolf Allers and Oswald Schwartz confounded Individual Psychology to a large mass of people. Shortly after this public lecture in 1927, Frankl, known to associate with Oswald and Allers, was removed from the Individual Psychology Union at the request of Alfred Adler himself.

Moving forward, in 1929 Frankl decided to create counseling services for adolescents in Vienna. Two years following his removal from the Individual Psychology Union, he chose to enter the public sector in response to an alarmingly high suicide rate in adolescents. What he noticed was children and young adults were committing suicide the day before, day of and day after the release of reports cards. Working out of his parent's apartment complex, in 1931 Frankl was able to contribute to a year without any adolescent suicides (Batthyany 2010). In light of this accomplishment, the local newspapers provided Frankl with the credit giving him some higher level of popularity in the psychological society. Following that, the tenets of Logotherapy became more thoroughly developed and Frankl discovered what he would describe as, "the awareness to not live meaninglessly" (Frankl 1967). This principle was observed and implemented throughout his work with the counseling services for adolescents and later on in the Steinhoff psychiatric clinic; in which Viktor claimed this principle helped treat neurotic patients, unemployed youth and suicidal clients. Even whilst working with patients between 1933 and 1939 that were diseased and had seemingly less control over their lives than the average person, these people were not deprived of their spiritual freedom. Frankl captured this idea with the word pathoplastic, defined as: "the retained ability of diseased person's to shape (up to a certain point) the nature of their symptoms, or to mold an existence that had been overshadowed by a psychological illness" (Frankl 1967). Throughout this work, he began to almost completely stray away from the psychoanalytic and individual psych background he was exposed to, and began to genuinely understand and observe each patient to solidify his overall conceptualization of man and therapeutic approach to treat such man. In thereof, Frankl posed the question as: "whether or not- and if so, to what extent- the patients were ready to make use of their relative freedom" (Frankl 1967). By holding this perspective, Frankl somewhat tested two major concepts of Logotherapy. The first concept was illustrated by becoming aware of human beings' ability to suffer in the face of an unchangeable fate. The second concept displayed is the ability of a person to cope with difficult life circumstances; essentially their Will to Meaning. The most importantt piece to understanding this philosophical concept is being cognizant that bearing such difficulties in life is worthwhile "because there is a 'More' through which suffering becomes acceptable" (Batthyany 2010).

Going off of that, it's important to mention that the second fundamental assumption of man- the Will to Meaning- is best pondered by viewing it as an oversimplification of Freud's will to pleasure and Adler's will to power. During the year of 1939, Frankl released a paper on the spiritual problems of psychotherapy and coined the term Existential Analysis. Here came a firmer structure of Logotherapy's roots, especially the advocating of such theory. All while, Frankl made the decision to falsify diagnoses for particular Jewish patients to prevent their persecution in concentration camps (Batthyany 2010). Frankl's Will to Meaning was, in a sense, accomplished during this time period because he recognized a balance between his will to power as a practicing doctor and his will to pleasure by avoiding the concentration camps himself. As a result, Frankl was able to discover a larger meaning for himself by helping others. Although this discovery process did not come without certain challenges; particularly during his visits from a Gestapo man.

In the midst of Frankl breaching ethical and legal codes as a doctor by falsifying diagnoses, he learned to put aside his bias against any person that was part of the Nazi regime for the sake of his clients and himself. One instance of Frankl's life that speaks to his impressive resiliency is when he provided what can be considered in vivo counseling to said Gestapo man. In 1941. Frankl was graced with a visit from this man who was enforcing Hitler's rule; but ended up holding a long discussion with Viktor involving a friend's personal issues. What was most interesting about this interaction of non-formal therapy is that the client- said Gestapo man- created an I-he relationship during the session, rather than the traditional I-thou. Hence, the individual was able to disclose certain personal information to Frankl as if the information was not his own, but a friends. By the end of this discussion, the Gestapo man showed great appreciation and thanked Frankl for the insight to share with his friend (Frankl

1967). This was most intriguing to Frankl because even though the person did not admit the issues were his own, it seemed, at least on the surface, that the in vivo session was beneficial.

After his time falsifying diagnoses at the Steinhoff Psychiatric Clinic, he was forced to give up his own private practice on the basis of Nazi race laws. Throughout the next three years, he was the Chief Physician for Neurology at the Rothschild Hospital of the Israelite Cultural Municipality (Batthyany 2010). In response to performing his duties as chief physician for neurology, he and his family were granted avoidance of the persecution of the Nazi's concentration camps. That is until 1942.

Earlier in the year of 1942, Viktor Frankl wrote and completed (for the time being) the book 'The Doctor and the Soul;' and within the context of that book his commitment to hope is illuminated. Frankl described his commitment to hope as: "the antidote to suicide, even when any hope of a way out is ostensibly hope for a miracle" (Batthyany 2010). This mindset was very much tested and put into perspective when he and his family were sent to a concentration camp called Theresienstadt. There are many stories of Frankl's time spent in the concentration camps over the next three years of his life; the most intriguing feat he conquered though was the ability to not only survive, but thrive in such a setting. He was able to thrive in reference to his creation of Shock-Squads. Shock-Squads brought together other doctors, rabbis and any other volunteers that would serve the purpose of mobile psychological counseling stations aiding prisoners in the concentration camp. In the midst of such a cruel and morbid experience for an individual to undergo, Frankl managed to remain dedicated to hope; or in other words, have unconditional hope. "He supported his argument for hope in difficult memories of despair by his own stance and perhaps more significantly trying to help others" (Batthyany 2010). Once again, Viktor Frankl is displaying resilience against external factors and is interestingly valuing oneself by recognizing and acting upon his capability to help others in their time of need.

By 1945, the Nazi Regime had managed to take away both of Viktor's parents, his mother in-law, his brother, his wife and his first manuscript of The Doctor and the Soul. What is most upsetting about these losses is he did not discover that his wife had passed away until a few days following her death. In the midst of all of this occurring, thoughts of his wife and her choice to stay with him until their eventual separation in the concentration camps is largely what Frankl gives credit for his ability to persist. Persistence, even to the point where he volunteered to go to another camp by the name of Turkheim to serve as a doctor treating typhus fever; in which he ended up contracting and overcoming. Eventually, gaining his liberation from the Nazi Regime through the efforts of American troops on April 27th, 1945 (Batthyany 2010). And yet, he continued to work as the appointed camp doctor for a military hospital at the Bavarian Health Resort of Bad Worishofen. In the face of redundancy, it must be reiterated that Frankl maintained throughout his time in concentrations camps, and continued to maintain until his death in 1997, a credence to the idea of having unconditional hope. Hope, being a deeper connection to the noological realm of existence. Hope, capturing the spiritual enlightenment he endured through such cruel and difficult life circumstances; ultimately avoiding the existential vacuum, yet embracing it's potentiality through the use of humor to facilitate unconditional hope. Therefore, not only did Frankl completely avoid "the experience of a total lack, or loss of an ultimate meaning to one's existence;" (Frankl 1967) but cherished the imbalance of equilibrium within himself and within the world.

S-FACTOR AND LOGOTHERAPY

Logotherapy, from a theoretical stance, is vibrant with knowledge on its own; but the piece that is necessary to explore in accordance with the S-Factor Theory is the idea of the spiritual unconscious. As Taccarino has indicated, the S-Factor does not bring an individual in itself greater life meaning and success, but allows the person to pursue it more effectively (Taccarino et al. 2015). This pursuit is rooted in the perceptual and spiritual level of choice, something Frankl captures as the noetic dimension. He makes the claim that the noetic dimension is, "considered the site of authentically human phenomenon such as love, humor or gratitude and distinguishes human beings from other animals" (Frankl 1967). This point of epitomizing the noetic/spiritual dimension of a person's reality is exactly what makes Logotherapy and Frankl's understanding of the world so profound and builds directly into the Success Drive/Self-Potency characteristic of the S-Factor Theory. Taking this stance towards understanding man's existence is pertinent when conceptualizing the three fundamental philosophical assumptions of humankind: Freedom of Will, Will to Meaning and Meaning of Life. Most importantly, this stance is key when applying these fundamental assumptions to the tenets of the S-Factor Theory.

For the purpose of this chapter, these three fundamental assumptions will have to be briefly defined to outline the comparison to the S-Factor Theory. Freedom of Will, Will to Meaning and Meaning of life are the general existential assumptions that Viktor Frankl (1967) claims is the basis for the overall discussion that occurs during the therapeutic process. In addition to these philosophical assumptions, there are three therapeutic techniques that Frankl epitomized that go hand in hand with applying the S-Factor theory in a practical matter.

To begin, the three therapeutic techniques discussed here are: Paradoxical Intention, Attitude modification and Dereflection. The first therapeutic technique of Logotherapy referred to as Paradoxical Intention, is the most applicable technique and exemplifies this first philosophical assumption (Freedom of Will); the idea that an individual always has the choice or even the control to configure their attitude in any context or conditions (Frankl 1967). Paradoxical Intention though, is the idea of, "self-distancing through humor or absurdity" (Ameli & Dattilio 2013). In doing so, the client or individual is able to break free of the vicious cycle of anxiety and almost demean the reluctancy towards any task or stressor. An example comes from an individual being afraid of speaking in public or giving a presentation; such as, "I can't wait for people to be entirely disinterested in my presentation, not laugh at any of my jokes and ridicule me for choosing such a topic to present on." In essence, the purpose of this technique is for the absurd statement to change the attitude of the client; then in turn reduce the symptom they wished to exonerate. Or as Ameli and Dattilo (2010) describes, "it counteracts anticipatory anxiety by having a reciprocal impact on the symptoms and thus breaking anxiety's vicious circle." This particular therapeutic technique is not exactly present in most other theories of psychotherapy and adds a bit of zest to Logotherapy. In addition, Frankl (2010) even made the claim that by using humor as part of the therapeutic process, it actually made Logotherapy less of a behavioral approach. With that said, some aspects of Paradoxical Intention do reflect some behavioral techniques such as exposure, flooding and satiation. Ascher (1989), "shares the opinion that some of the techniques developed in the frame of behavior therapy, mainly imposition and satiation, are simply the 'translation of paradoxical intention'." Ascher here makes quite a bit of sense, but the biggest difference between these behavioral techniques and Frankl's Paradoxical Intention is that Frankl is approaching the client with an existential lens; rather than focusing particularly on the behavior. Not only Frankl has considered this though! In more recent empirical studies, the technique of Paradoxical Intention has been validated with helping individuals with sleep disorders, agoraphobia, public-speaking anxiety, and quitting smoking cigarettes (Ascher 1989, Schulenberg & Melton 2008, & Fabry 2010). One case study even found paradoxical intention therapy to be useful in treating refractory nonepileptic events (Chapleau et al. 2013). In thereof, the efficacy of Paradoxical Intention in a sense 'transcends' a behavioral technique beyond the behavioral aspect of the technique. Although, the claim here is that this is a technique that can be practiced by everyone; not just helping professionals.

When applied to the S-Factor, this technique is an activity a person is able to utilize without the help of a counselor/therapist. In reference to Self-Valuing, one can make the best of any situation by finding a humorous perspective to view it through. Instead of ruminating over a stressful event or a poor decision, or even failing to reach a certain goal in your life (such as while playing The Road to Success game); an individual can place more focus on how silly or humorous their decision making process was. In addition, recognizing that the first four personality characteristics play directly into the success drive/self-potency characteristic, it's helpful to notice that Paradoxical Intention can facilitate this change in perspective. Humor can both relax and excite an individual and thus make them more motivated, give them more energy, be more persistent and essentially help discover more joy in their lives. The discovery process of joy in one's life is a salient concept between the S-Factor Theory and Logotherapy. Reaching back to the spiritual unconscious, Frankl believed that "the very pursuit of happiness thwarts happiness; happiness cannot be pursued. It must ensue" (Frankl 1967). I make this point here to emphasize the idea that the spiritual unconscious is largely an unconscious concept; as well as being something a person must act upon as much as think about. Overall, it is based upon hope. One thing that Frankl considers as a central tenant to Logotherapy and to man's overall existence is the idea of hope. And this is not just the overused term of hope found in the motivational pictures across the internet; this is considered unconditional hope. Unconditional hope to Viktor Frankl is captured in a quote discussing his book, *The Doctor and the Soul*, involving his time spent in concentration camps during World War II. That quote is,

"Frankl's commitment to hope as the antidote to suicide, even when any hope of a way out is ostensibly hope for a miracle. In fact, this unconditional hope also preserves the argument for the unconditional meaningfulness of existence, including the possibility of retroactively reclaiming meaning from the *tragic triad* of pain, guilt and death" (Batthyany & Tallon 2010).

Hope is a concept that is embraced by the masses, was especially embraced by Frankl, and is a force to be reckoned with when built into the S-Factor Theory.

The next question posed is how to adapt the S-Factor theory to accommodate for this unconditional hope. What's most prosperous about the S-Factor Theory is that hope is somewhat already accounted for with the term of habituated intention. By holding the correct, or virtuous, attitude with the intent to change, along with acting upon this intent- an individual has quite possibly endless opportunities. Frankl captures the idea of habituated intention in the third fundamental assumption of man as meaning of life. Lewis (2011) conceptualized that there are three different ways to discover the meaning of life: creative value, experiential value and attitudinal value. The creative value is what we give to the world in terms of accomplishing a task, doing a good deed or creating work; as compared to Internal Motivation and Self-Regulation and in some ways Interpersonal Effectiveness. Experiential value, also labeled as what we take from this world, is the experience of truth, beauty and love toward another human being (Lewis 2011); as compared to Affective Effectiveness and somewhat Interpersonal Effectiveness. Then attitudinal value reflects the stand one takes toward unchangeable situations or unavoidable suffering; which is similar to the behavior one takes on to gather a large Success Drive. In short, Frankl's understanding of the meaning of life can be captured as what we give to the world, what we take from the world and the stand we take in this world. When viewed through the S-Factor Theory, with a Logotherapeutic lens, meaning of life is captured in three different ways. How we motivate and regulate ourselves to give to the world (and others), how we shape and experience our affect towards the world, and how we think and act upon our success drive.

The second therapeutic technique of Logotherapy is Attitude Modification. This technique reflects the philosophical assumption of the Will to Meaning; which is the idea of striving to make your life meaningful. Attitude Modification is put simply as a guided discovery process. As an individual explores the available perspectives, opinions, attitudes and actions they have available in understanding their own life, they become aware of the idea of searching for a greater purpose. This is particularly accomplished through Socratic dialogue with another person or group of individuals. If a space to explore meaningful values is provided to someone, they can then understand this concept at greater depth. Only then can a person begin to create an action plan to change their attitude towards life; and specifically their own life. In Cognitive Behavior Therapy (CBT), Judith Beck (2011) captures this process in a practical matter with something referred to as the Dysfunctional Thought Record. Here a person is able to visibly log particular situations in life, automatic thoughts that occur during those situations, and the emotions one experiences attached to said thoughts. Once these three items are recorded down, a person is then able to write down alternative/adaptive responses to these situations and rate the outcome of both the adaptive response and their normal response. For more information involving this worksheet, refer to the book Cognitive Behavior Therapy: *Basic and Beyond* (2011). The difference between CBT and Logotherapy though, is Logotherapy intends to first attend to the **attitude** of the client, and then create behavior modification. Once the individual indulges in this Socratic dialogue, activation of the will to meaning will effortlessly lead to behavior modification and facilitate the client's attempt to avoid the existential vacuum. As Frankl would be led to believe, this technique can be used to thwart the issues of guilt, loss, grief, suffering, serious diseases or mental illnesses, neurosis and depression. The point being, once someone has shifted their attitude towards their dysfunctional thought or symptom only then will they be more open to creating change within their own lives.

Lastly, the therapeutic technique to be discussed is Dereflection; in which "shifts the client's attention away from the symptom and redirects it toward another person or a motivating/meaningful goal" (Ameli & Dattilio 2013). Lukas (et al. 1981) claims that this process of Dereflection has four sequences: self-transcendence, finding meaningful goals and tasks, symptom reduction and change in attitude. First off, self-transcendence and finding meaningful goals is exactly what internal motivation and self-regulation are pitching. Once the first two steps are accomplished, the individual is able to treat their experiences of affective effectiveness and interpersonal effectiveness as opportunities to reduce their symptoms; to an extent, due to it being a process that is endured not completed. In more practical terms, self-transcendence is used to generate activities that are **pleasant** and **meaningful** considering the clients personal values. Focusing on the pleasant and meaningful piece of this technique is taking into account the creative, experiential, and attitudinal values; the key components to the third philosophical assumption of Meaning of Life. It is important to mention though, that when assisting clients (or in this case yourself) in finding these meaningful tasks and goals, the key suggestion is to physically write said task and goals down. In an effort to promote well-being and enduring change, having a physical copy for the individual to reflect on and have readily available can be most beneficial.

After completing the first two steps in Dereflection, the person will develop the necessary skills to persist in those and other meaningful life goals. Following that, they must act upon these goals and tasks to create a reduction in unwanted symptoms and thus change their attitude about their behavior. In thereof, a person can change their attitude to begin to develop a stronger value of themselves and hence create a higher success drive. Now, although these four steps combined with the S-Factor personality traits seem to work interdependently- there is one piece missing. As mentioned in an earlier section, the idea of being successful is made up of the many operationally defined character elements that Taccarino describes in the S-Factor Theory; but does not account for the term *meaningful success*. Whether it be related to a person's career, individual aspirations, familial aspirations or anything else in life; residing in the feeling that your actions are worthwhile and have a greater meaning is something Frankl would claim every person strives towards or at the very least conceptualizes on some level. In the S-Factor Theory, meaningful success is somewhat described when discussing the four elements of: internal motivation, self-valuing, affective effectiveness and interpersonal effectiveness.

Outside of operationally defining meaningful success in the S-Factor literature, there is genuinely much overlap between the theories. Aforementioned, epitomizing the noetic/spiritual of a person's reality is exactly what makes Logotherapy and Frankl's understanding of the world so profound and builds directly into the Success Drive/Self-Potency characteristic of the S-Factor

Theory. Combined with the three fundamental assumptions of humankind (Freedom of Will, Will to Meaning & Meaning of Life), tenets of the S-Factor Theory can grow exponentially. Overall, Viktor Frankl has created and contributed much insight towards the philosophical and the therapeutic breadth of knowledge. With his information and S-the Taccarino-Leonard Factor Theory, there is a significant amount of intervention strategies that can be created in academic, professional and personal settings to produce a higher success drive.

INTERNAL MOTIVATION & SELF-REGULATION

From the perspective of a clinician, there are a few key themes that seem to be illuminated already in Frankl's lifespan. First off, there are a lot of tendencies within his behavior that exemplify his internal motivation. The fact that Viktor was able to jump directly into practice at a community based level is extraordinary. Also, this plays into the success drive of Viktor having a strong work ethic and need to succeed. In addition, Frankl exemplified a high level of self-regulation during his time working in the Individual Psychology Union. He established what his life meaning was, in a sense, and he created personal goals without much external direction from his peers and mentors. In fact, he has shown resilience to the fundamental beliefs of Adlerian Psychology and persistence in his own beliefs that, at that point in history, refuted mainstream psychological society. Most interestingly, Frankl is embracing his own fundamental assumption of the Freedom of Will. Even though he had ventured down the path that did not align with his own personal beliefs and values, he recognized his freedom to choose his attitude towards this event and take a stand towards his conditions.

For an individual to define their life meaning and their goals, it is necessary to motivate oneself without the requirement of much external direction. External direction can be compared to using a punishment and reward system to help reinforce a person to achieve such goals and configure their life meaning. Although, making this claim does not serve the purpose of disproving behaviorist theories. Instead, it recognizes that external motivation is not the primary form of motivation that can make an individual successful. Deci and Ryan (1985) stated, "some intentional behaviors are initiated and regulated through choice as an expression of oneself, whereas other intentional behaviors are pursued and coerced by intrapsychic and environmental forces and thus do not represent true choice." Here Deci and Ryan provide the example accommodating the idea that not all decisions are made distinctively through our own choice. In thereof, when an individual epitomizes internal motivation, a worldview is created that promotes self-actualization, personal becoming and thus trains he or she to self-regulate. And once again, self-actualization and self-regulation are two terms that Frankl would describe collectively as self-transcendence (Ameli & Datillio 2013); which also plays into the 'will to meaning' (Frankl 1967).

The following is an editorial comment from Dr. Taccarino: "My concept of habituated intention as a basis for strengthening an individual's S-Factor is consistent with Frankl's theory and the importance of internal motivation and self-regulation as bases for achieving a meaningful form of success readiness. I contend that if S-Factor transformation is to occur it is necessary for a person to be aware of the elements of his/her S-Factor and to make an intentional and meaningful commitment to building the habits of thinking and acting that are consistent with a strong S-Factor. The importance of meaningful intention appears common to Frankl's explanation of self-transcendence and my view of habituated intention. Essentially the accomplishment of S-Factor transformation via habituated intention can lead to a form of positive self- transcendence. "

SELF VALUING

Self-Valuing is one concept that has not been covered as thoroughly during this chapter, and rather, has focused on Frankl helping other people. That is not to say he had little value of himself though. There are two main aspects of Frankl's personality that have stuck out thus far that show his level of self-value. Those being: his altruistic attitude and his unconditional hope. During his time spent in the concentration camps, thoughts of his wife and working on his manuscript of "The Doctor and The Soul "were two key factors that kept him faithful. He remained unconditionally dedicated to the hope of his life continuing, the hope that each day was worth living and especially the hope that he would someday be with his wife again. Not only that, but Frankl felt respected and worthy of success due to his own transcendent thoughts; as well as through the reciprocity he received from clients, the psychological society (in later years), his peers and through the relationships he pursued throughout his time in the concentration camps.

Frankl's time spent in the concentration camps was an extremely insightful, yet terrible experience. Although, he still remained altruistic. By being forced against your will to undergo such scrutinization and still remain resistant and have such a deep care for others is unbelievable. As mentioned in an earlier section, his decision to treat typhus fever patients, contract and overcome typhus fever and then continue on to treat these patients is quite ludicrous. All of these examples lead to one point though: Viktor felt so comfortable and competent in his ability to help others. Not only that, but he acted upon his ability. In fact, one might say he could be somewhat pompous in his existential analysis of man. In a very positive and insightful perspective, but as stated before also pompous, Frankl made the claim that "neurotic patients cannot be happy because they have not grown into life, because they despise it, devalue it and hate it" (Frankl 1967). This perspective is quite enlightening and intriguing. Most importantly, it brings attention to Viktor's unconditional hope towards the altruistic ability of humankind; that is of course including himself.

AFFECTIVE EFFECTIVENESS

Moving forward, the third element is described as affective effectiveness and can be conceptualized as emotional learning. "Affective effectiveness involves a type of emotional maturity that is the foundation for impulse control, resilience, social adaptability, self-governance and the ability to generate enthusiasm for achieving goals for both oneself and others" (Taccarino 2014). This captures the other end of the spectrum in comparison to self-valuing, in that one must will learn to love others once they are able to value and love themselves. Frankl's dedication to the altruistic ability of humankind recognizes his true appreciation and understanding of others. Also, his social adaptability to generate enthusiasm is metaphorically contagious. Before the time of World War II, Frankl chose to create his own counseling services for adolescents. His ability to understand and get through to children and young adults that were committing suicide in response to their report card grades is a true testament of his affect. Even the local newspaper credited him for being one of the main reasons the adolescent suicide rate went to zero in Vienna during 1931. What's most interesting about this accomplishment is his divergent thinking that allowed him to pay attention to the link between report card grades and the timing of the majority of the adolescent suicides.

Ultimately, this creative thinking is a trait of Frankl's that existed back when he was studying Adlerian Psychology. Without his decision to move away from his Adlerian and Psychoanalytic background, one can claim he may have never ventured into the public sector to assist suicidal patients in such a manner. In doing so, he was provided with a fantastic setting that facilitated a process of true observational learning through a practitioner's lens. Frankl even admitted to this during his own process of discovering what motivates humankind and attempting to create a meaningful lifestyle of his own. This humbleness he encompassed is a trait that leads straight into and supports his ability to relate to others.

INTERPERSONAL EFFECTIVENESS

Not only has Frankl learned to value others and himself, but can promote his own and others creative and divergent ideas. A mindset such as this plays into the next character element that is interpersonal effectiveness. This element converges on the ideas that an individual gains the ability to persuasively and effectively communicate his or her own ideas; while also finding enjoyment in social interactions and feeling somewhat accepted by their peers. Without this ability, the individual will appear as continuously being on the brink of acting upon a potentially creative and divergent idea. They will not display the demeanor of someone that is poised in their thoughts or social interactions. Instead, Viktor Frankl showed exemplary interpersonal effectiveness with another creation of his; that being Shock-Squads. As mentioned earlier, the Shock-Squads brought together other doctors, rabbis and any other volunteers with the aim to aid fellow prisoners in the concentration camp. These mobile psychological counseling stations exemplified his skills in interpersonal understanding, as well as how effective he was at expressing his interpersonal understanding. After being labeled somewhat of a hero in Vienna with his work with adolescents, he then went on to completely resist the mental anguish that came with being a prisoner of war. He not only survived, but thrived during this time. Choosing to still continue to practice his professional work and be concerned with the lives of his fellow species, as well as conjure up a lucrative idea such as group counseling on the move is impressive in itself. Then, to further build off of his interpersonal effectiveness, he managed to convince others to join him and to continually motivate them that there was still hope and purpose for their lives. Overall, Frankl managed to thrive particularly well in the category of interpersonal effectiveness, and displays the other three of internal motivation, self-valuing and affective effectiveness very well. All of these characteristics are converging together within Frankl to create quite a large S-Factor; therefore his self-potency is next to be discussed.

SELF POTENCY & SUCCESS DRIVE

Success Drive consists of someone that is self-motivated, resilient, ambitious and persistent in the face and action of failure (Taccarino 2014). Along with that, self-potency is broken down into a social and an internal category. The social category describes the level of energy, spontaneity, hope, joy of life, ambition and excitement one displays. Then the internal category is the inner confidence, pervasive goodness, and soul, quality of character, spirituality and courage a person displays. There are many factors that define a success drive and also very much overlap between the S-Factor Theory and Logotherapy; hope, courage and resilience are the three that seem most apparent. To fully understand the operations of the success drive, it's key to take into consideration this statement from Taccarino: "Hope and self-valuing are the engines of the success drive, depreciation and discouragement are its flat tires" (Taccarino 2015). This quote captures the S-Factor theory into a more concrete image of motivation and determination that can thoroughly contribute to the understanding of lifespan development.

REFERENCES

Ameli, M., Dattilio, F. M. (2013). Enhancing CBT with Logotherapy: techniques for clinical practice. *Journal of Psychotherapy*, 50(3) 387-391. doi: 10.1037/a0033394

Ascher, L. M. (Ed.) (1989). *The therapeutic paradox*. New York: Guilford Press.

Beck, J. S. (2011). Identifying and Modifying Intermediate Beliefs. In J. S. Beck (Ed.),

Cognitive Behavior Therapy: Basics and Beyond. (pp. 198-227). New York, NY: The Guilford Press.

Deci, E. L., & Ryan, R. M. (1985). *Intrinsic motivation and self-determination in human behavior*. New York: Plenum Press.

Chapleau, K.M., Landsberger, S.A., Povlinski, J. & Diaz, D.R. (2013). Using Paradoxical

Intention Therapy to Treat Refractory Nonepileptic Events. *The Academy of Psychosomatic Medicine, 54*, 398-401.

Fabry, D. D. S. (2010). Evidence base for paradoxical intention: Reviewing clinical outcome studies. *The International Forum for Logotherapy, 33,* 21–29.

Frankl, V. E. (2010). *The feeling of meaninglessness: A challenge to psychotherapy and philosophy*. A. Batthyany & A. Tallon (Eds.). Milwaukee, WI: Marquette University Press.

Frankl, V. E. (1967). *Psychotherapy and Existentialism: Selected papers on Logotherapy.* Long Island, New York: Washington Square Press, Inc.

Lewis, M. H. (2011). Defiant power: An overview of Viktor Frankl's Logotherapy and existential analysis, PDF version.

Retrieved from www.defiantpower.com. Retrieved May 18, 2015.

Lukas, E. (1981). New ways for Dereflection. *The International Forum for Logotherapy, 4,* 13-28.

Schulenberg, S. E., & Melton, A. M. A. (2008). On the measure of meaning: Logotherapy's empirical contributions to Humanistic psychology. *The Humanistic Psychologist, 36,* 21–44.

Szameitat, D. P., Szameitat, A. J., Wildgruber, D., Dietrich, S., Alter, K., Darwin, C. J., & Sterr, A. (2009). Differentiation of emotions in laughter at a behavioral level. *American Psychological Association: Emotion, 9*(3), 397-405. doi: 10.1037/a0015692

Taccarino, J. *Success readiness development* [PDF document]. Retrieved from Lecture Notes Online Website: https://d2l. depaul.edu/d2l/le/content/349634/viewContent/2511972/ Vie

Taccarino, J. et al, (2015). The Taccarino-Leonard S(Success)-Factor: *The Psychological Roots of Success.* , Melbourne, Florida: *Motivational Press*

Trautwein, U., Marsh, H. W., Nagengast, B., Ludtke, O., Nagy, G., & Jonkmann, K. (2012). Probing for the multiplicative term in modern expectancy-value theory: A latent interaction modeling study. *Journal of Educational Psychology, 104*(3), 763-777. doi: 10.1037/a0027470

CHAPTER 4

THE S-FACTOR AND ONLINE EDUCATION

By An Chi Cheng and Joseph Cheng

This chapter addresses online learning environments and discusses how the S-Factor can help instructors assist students to achieve success in online education. The chapter was co-authored by Dr. An Chih Cheng, Associatet Professor in the College of Education at DePaul University, and Joseph Cheng, a psychologist and business consultant..

CRITICAL PEDAGOGICAL ISSUES OF ONLINE COURSES

Over the past couple decades, online education has transcended traditional brick-and-mortar classrooms to virtual classrooms where teaching and learning can take place anytime, anywhere. With the increasing availability of high-speed Internet, online learning opportunities have rapidly expanded, ranging from delivering corporate training and continuing professional development, to pursuing advanced degrees in higher education. Currently, it is estimated more than six million students take at least one online course. In addition, a high proportion of academic and administration leaders believe online education is critical to long-term development. It is often assumed that online education is capable of bringing out effective teaching, improving students' achievement, and democratizing education, at least for everyone who has access to the Internet. It is also widely claimed that online education would transform education at all levels. Unfortunately, such a scenario has not happened. For example, in higher education the experiments of Massive Open Online Courses (MOOCs), which promise to provide higher education opportunities to everyone, have failed: MOO courses tend to have low course completion rates and few students earn passing grades. In addition, studies (e.g. CREDO, 2011) have shown that students enrolled in online K-12 schools performed worse academically and were more likely to repeat a grade than their counterparts in traditional classrooms.

So, what went wrong? First, from a cognitive perspective, there is a misplaced faith of adopting autonomous technology in teaching and learning environments. Currently online course designers and instructors believe that because students have access to computers, and because computers can deliver pre-programmed course materials (e.g. quizzes or pre-recorded lectures), students therefore can learn anytime, anywhere. However, content delivery should not be confused with meaningful learning. Pre-made online materials are presented a linear, prescriptive, and mechanical fashion that disregards an individual's prior knowledge and social experience. Reducing experiential learning to a mode of conditioning is like a Skinner's behaviorism box where a mouse learns to push the lever to receive a food reward or to avoid punishment. Behaviorism sees learning as the product of stimuli, not a process of active thinking. In other words, education is not car manufacturing. Both individuals' prior backgrounds and their social contexts must be recognized and appreciated if meaningful learning is to take place.

Second, from a pedagogical perspective, there is a misnomer in using the term of individualized curriculum. As discussed above, in order to maximize economic efficiency, online content is static, premade material that takes a one-size-fits-all approach. Online courses thus address to no one and knows nothing about the students. Students taking the online courses then feel disconnected, become unmotivated and then fail to complete the online tasks. It is important to know that learning is always a social experience (Vygotsky, 1978), not an individual task. Learning requires motivation, affection, self-regulation, and interpersonal effectiveness that emerge only in a meaningful social context. Therefore, online course designers and instructors need to be cognizant about how to create a social learning community in each online course, and how to build such a social context with new technology, but not led by technology.

Designing A Successful Online Learning Environment

Knowing the flaws of current online courses, we therefore need to find a way to rectify it. We will achieve this goal by incorporating success factors into online course design and teaching. The core S-Factor traits of interpersonal effectiveness, self- valuing, internal motivation and self-regulation, affective effectiveness, self-potency and success drive can serve as a meaningful guideline to this end. We will discuss each trait in detail and illustrate how they can help to build and teach a successful online course.

Interpersonal Effectiveness

Students of the digital generation are well versed in technology. They are "connected online" at all times, from posting messages on social media to consuming online content in their "connected car." However, knowing how to use digital technology does not necessarily transfer to knowing how to learn something meaningfully. For example, although students are capable of posting and exchanging short instant messages in quick succession, studies have found that students may lack formal communication skills; such as, the ability to write longer arguments that demonstrate critical thinking skills (Feiertag & Berge, 2008). A student may have great ideas, but unless the student can communicate the value of the idea to others in a socially effective way, success can always be just beyond the horizon (Taccarino, 5). It is also reported that poor writing and communication skills resulting from self-focused social media use may negatively affect students' reading and comprehension skills in an academic context.

Hence, to be successful in online learning, it is important to start with a foundational approach: by transforming students' online media skills into academically beneficial interpersonal effectiveness. Interpersonal effectiveness stresses the ability to relate to people on a person-to-person level, and build enthusiasm and commitment from people on a large scale, media based level. This requires students to shift self-centered postings into focusing on developing the ability to articulate lengthy, cohesive, and critical arguments. This transformative work is not an easy task. It requires students to constantly reflect on themselves and relate their thoughts to others via *habituated intention*. From there, students will also build true confidence that is not superficial. Acquiring such a self-assurance in a meaningful social context has long term positive impact on both academic work and future careers.

Internal Motivation and Self-Regulation

Effective interpersonal use of digital technology thus prepares students to develop psychological and academic readiness to achieve success in online learning environments. The next step then is to sustain such intention and ability. This requires strong internal motivation and self-regulation, and these two success traits directly address the most common problems of online learning: that students enrolled in online courses tend to be unmotivated, complete less of the required work, and achieve lower overall academic performance.

Motivation theories tell us that individuals are more likely to succeed when they are internally motivated, rather than prompted by external rewards or punishments (Ryan & Deci, 2000). Thus, an online course designer should aim to facilitate the development of intrinsic motivation. This can be achieved by a dialectical approach. Instead of providing inflexible pre-made course objectives that are blind to students' backgrounds, online course designers need to build a system that 1) recognizes students as active learners who have their own sense of self and interest; 2) guides students to locate their internal core values and desires, and aligns them with the framework of the particular course being taught; 3) develops co-evolving learning plans that allow students' active exploration, needs fulfillment, and psychological growth. Such a social and adaptive approach provides a strong basis for self-actualization in online courses. Essentially, digital technology cannot be seen as a way to passively transmit facts. Instead, online courses need to be built in a way that foster active knowledge construction by doing, reflecting, and conversing with real-world stimulation and interaction.

Internal motivation and self- regulation go hand-in-hand. Internal motivation leads to self-regulation. Although online courses are self-paced and save students time, such as time otherwise spent on commuting, online students do not always manage time well. Although external reminders can be useful, the problem is often due to lack of motivation. When students are motivated internally, they are more likely to become active learners, and are more able and willing to self-regulate impulses and distractions that could block learning. When students feel more capable in doing online work, this in turn promotes self-confidence and increases their academic performance. The interactive nature of digital technology then provides opportunities for students for further engagement and contribution to the online learning community.

Self-Potency, Self-Valuing, and Success Drive

Those positive academic traits then trigger upward spirals toward academic success and enhanced psychological well-being. When students find their self-actualization aligns with and can be achieved in the online course, they project a powerful trajectory that leads not only to the success of the particular online course, but their academic goal. This is an active teaching approach that requires the collaboration from both course instructors and students. This is a positive learning experience that leads students to the manifestation of self-valuing, inner confidence and pursuit of pervasive goodness.

Helping students to develop and sustain self-drive can be achieved in two categories: an internal approach and a social approach. First, online course designers are encouraged to implement cues or checklists that prompt individual students check their own goals, examine their own work, and develop new targets on a weekly basis during the course. Such an individualized guidance allows students to stay on track and complete required tasks. The sense of accomplishment then leads to the development of confidence, courage and resilience. Second, online course designers should also create a space for students to engage in social activities with instructors and peers. For example, online discussion forums and video conferences. Such a space provides students the opportunity to interact, reflect, and challenge ideas and beliefs. It also allows students to assume group responsibility and develop leadership skills. Online instructors should mediate such online interaction to ensure it attains a high level of energy, spontaneity, joy, and ambition that ultimately contributes to the expansion of students' knowledge base and higher success drive.

Affective Effectiveness

Affection is a critical topic that is often ignored in online course design and teaching. Successful learning depends upon an individual's enthusiasm about the topic and shared interpersonal relationships. A student's emotion can positively or negatively affect their learning experience to a great degree. Thus learning cannot be devoid of affection or social context. In other words, online learning cannot be considered as an individual task. There is a need to recognize students' emotional needs and to motivate students to relate to others in both cognitive and affective dimensions. Yet, as online courses aim to make learning mechanical, it is not surprising that they fail to make students want to learn. The notion of affection effectiveness aims to remedy this situation.

Specifically, affective effectiveness involves a type of emotional maturity that is the foundation for impulse control, resilience, social adaptability, self-governance and the ability to generate an enthusiasm for achieving goals both for oneself and others. In the online context, this means that the online courses need to be designed and taught in a way that help students to learn emotional confidence and maturity. This makes sense especially when we have recognized that online courses are a social space, rather than individual work. For example, due to the false sense of anonymity of online communication, some students may be aggressive or disrespectful. This negatively affects others' emotions and learning becomes disruptive. Thus, even though people do not see each other in online courses, students need to be sensitive to the emotions of others and maintain civility in online courses. In this way, students are protected and online communication become intimate and connected. Positive emotion further allows students to solve complicated academic work, mitigate interpersonal problems, and support self-drive to succeed. By nurturing affective effectiveness and social adaptability, instructors facilitate interpersonal effectiveness, generate enthusiasm among students, and foster a positive learning environment. This also stresses the need for online instructors to be present and facilitate students' work in the online courses.

Conclusion

In this chapter we discussed several pedagogical issues and psychological bases of online education. We analyzed common problems and illustrated how the S-Factor may be used to solve these problems. It is important to note that, although S-Factor assessment can be used to mitigate existing problems, in order to help students to achieve their full potential, it is for the best that course designers develop online courses with the S-Factor in mind from the initial stage and that course instructors consistently implement S-Factor develoment when teaching.

REFERENCE

CREDO. (2011). Charter school performance in Pennsylvania. from Center for Research on Education Outcomes (CREDO) Stanford University http://credo.stanford.edu/reports/PA State Report 20110404 FINAL.pdf

Jeff Feiertag, Zane L. Berge, (2008) "Training Generation N: how educators should approach the Net Generation", Education + Training, Vol. 50 Iss: 6, pp.457 – 464

Ryan, R. M., & Deci, E. L. (2000). Self-determination theory and the facilitation of intrinsic motivation, social development, and well-being. *American Psychologist, 55,* 68-78.

Vygotsky, L. (1978). Mind in society: The development of higher psychological process. Cambridge, MA: Harvard University Press.

PART 2

Case Study Insights into the Developmental and Educational Uses and Applications of the theory of the S-Factor

CHAPTER 5

SELF CASE STUDY OF A GRADUATE STUDENT WHO LEARNED HOW TO SUCCEED BY USING THE STRENGTH OF HER S-FACTOR

This self case study was written by a graduate student in the College of Education at DePaul University who prefers to keep her identity anonymous. As an African American woman she provides insights into the workings of the S-Factor that I found to be very inspirational regarding how she used the strength of her S-Factor to overcome her personal handicaps and challenges.

According to Dr. Taccarino the S-Factor can vary in strength within an individual depending on the relative stimulation, development and maturation of these interrelated core elements: self –valuing; internal motivation and self regulation; affective effectiveness; interpersonal effectiveness; self-potency and success drive. Developing the S-Factor in individuals does not alter the inherited characteristics or talents of an individual, but a strong S-Factor can energize an individual to develop their abilities and help them to perform at the higher end of their potentials (Taccarino, Success Readiness Development pg. 1).

In my experience, I have found this to be true. When looking at my own S-Factor, I can see how the strength of my six core character and personality elements has served me well. Allow me to explain. I have never been a good standardized test taker nor was I very good at studying for prolonged periods of time. Thus, my standardized test scores as well as my grades never truly reflected my true intelligence, skills, and talents. Consequently, the fallout was this, while applying to college I was accepted under conditional status to the University of Wisconsin Oshkosh because my SAT scores and GPA average did not quite meet their requirement for enrollment. However, elements of my S-Factor—the extracurricular activities I was involved in, my unique experiences, my ability to articulate myself in my personal statement, taken together, allowed the university to see my potential and accept me for enrollment.

Unbeknownst to me, I had an issue with undiagnosed Attention Deficit Hyperactivity Disorder (ADHD), which was impacting my ability to academically achieve. Perhaps if the S-Factor assessment had been administered to me, my underlying learning disability would have been identified early on in my educational career. Unfortunately, I was left to deal with the challenges of my undiagnosed ADHD for 25 years. It wasn't until I had children of my own and they were diagnosed with the condition, that I saw a parallel between my educational experience and theirs. I decided to get assessed and it was confirmed that I too had the condition.

Had it not been for the strength of my S-Factor, I would not be writing this paper now. Even though it has taken me from 1991, when I graduated from undergrad and having dappled with attaining a Master's degree in Public Administration, until now to actualize my dream of becoming an educator focused on helping students who could find themselves in similar situations as me, it has been my strong S-Factor that has kept me plugging along and striving toward my goal. This is not to say that my core elements were all functioning at the same level of strength (due in large part to my condition of course).

Internal Motivation and Self-Regulation

My internal motivation and self-regulation was compromised by my ADHD. The level of my strength in this area can be qualified by the time it took for me to get to this point in my life given my undiagnosed condition. This is not to say that my strength in the key aspects of defining life meaning, self defined not other defined world view for self-actualization and personal becoming were compromised. In fact it was my high level of strength in this area that sustained me for the long haul. I have often been described as a high achiever because of the goals that I have set for myself and my achievement of them. Because of my condition, I developed a work ethic of persistence and the resilience that drove my internal motivation and self-regulation. My "won't quit" attitude serves me well—even now as I attend school full time, work full time, while raising three boys!

Self-Valuing

The element of self-valuing was high on the Richter scale for me as well. I was instilled with love, respect and success very early in life. My parents did an excellent job of allowing me to follow my pursuits of interest (i.e. Girl Scouts, the Theatre, reading books, multicultural and dynamic experiences) and a healthy understanding of my cultural background (I am a first generation African American born to immigrant parents. I had unique experiences that my fellow peers did not have. I could say that I have travelled to Africa, that my mother worked at the United Nations, that my father was educated in the United Kingdom, and that I have family members living in many parts of the world. I valued my unique sense of self. However, my self-valuing was slightly compromised by the fact that while people thought I was smart and I knew I was highly intelligent, my grades didn't always show it. Many of my peers assumed I was a straight A student and my teachers often said that I wasn't working up to my ability. My grades were not indicative of my talents and skills. I knew that it was a paradox but I didn't know why it was happening. After dropping out of grad school it took me a while to get the courage to return back to school. This wasn't until I received the ADHD diagnosis and began treatment for my condition. Not only did I gain an understanding of my condition but I also now had the tools to and supports to succeed in my educational endeavors. It was my self-valuing that helped me seek the help and support I needed to mitigate my diagnosis.

Affective Effectiveness

Under the conditions of my untreated ADHD, my affective effectiveness took a direct hit in my adulthood. While I was relatively emotionally balanced as a child, it wasn't until I was faced with taking care of my children, trying to figure out how to attain my life goals, and maintaining a healthy marriage, did my affective effectiveness start to wan. My emotional confidence was lacking and I began to self-medicate through the use of marijuana. The level of energy and the high stress brought on by trying to strive for perfection in the aforementioned areas of my life became arduous and self-defeating. It was easier to take the edge off and dull my senses a bit just to cope. Things really came to a head when I decided that I was going to go back to school and my self-medicating almost tipped the scale into full-blown addiction as I tried to figure out how I was going to do so. I grappled with a high level fear of failing. If not for my strong self-valuing and self-regulation, I may not have made the leap from addiction back to sobriety, and eventual enrollment in a master's degree program.

Affective effectiveness involves a type of emotional maturity that is the foundation of impulse control, resilience, social adaptability, self governance and the ability to generate an enthusiasm for achieving goals both for oneself and others (Taccarino pg. 4). I had to draw heavily on these already existing aspects of my character and the goals that I had for my family, in order to build up and strengthen my affective effectiveness. So how did I do this exactly? It was through the next element that I am about to discuss—Interpersonal Effectiveness.

Interpersonal Effectiveness

Interpersonal effectiveness is an essential component of the S-Factor. Moreover, self-valuing, affective effectiveness, and interpersonal effectiveness are heavily interrelated with the S-Factor (Taccarino pg. 4). Thankfully, my interpersonal effectiveness was developed at a very early age and I have no limitations in my self-assuredness and I enjoy social interactions. This aspect of my character greatly helped me strengthen my affective effectiveness. I began to actively speak with my peers and colleagues about my goals and aspirations in returning to school. I began to develop an educational framework that would help me reach my educational goals. I began to employ and share my creative and divergent thinking about what I wanted to do with my educational career. I decided that I wanted to help students, like myself, avoid the pitfalls that come with undiagnosed learning disabilities. I know what it takes to be an exceptional learner, I know how to manage being an exceptional learner, and I know what it looks and feels like when an exceptional learner fails to be diagnosed. I want to help parents and students achieve their potential.

My goal is to motivate the voiceless in our classrooms, advocate for increased and better resources for Special Education, and shift the perception of what it means to be an exceptional learner. I began to look at the many youth that I've come into contact with, as a social service provider, and understood that if they had the necessary supports and tools needed for their learning, they would be better equipped to navigate their educational journey. By pursuing a degree in Special Education it is my goal to gain skills that will enable me to develop assessment tools to further increase the accuracy with which we are able to meet the individual needs of our diverse student populations. Furthermore, I am interested in curriculum design and best practices in classroom operations for all learners and especially exceptional learners.

I began to further develop and support my ideas around like learner classrooms. Not to confuse this with the converse

Learning How to Succeed

of mainstreaming and inclusion but rather I am speaking of learning style. Students of the same learning style might be better served in an environment where their peers are able to relate to them academically and act as a support for them. Instruction provided in the best suited modality for similar learners in a classroom, will help teachers to develop lesson plans that can truly meet the needs of every student within his/her classroom, and additionally lend to efficient and effective instruction and knowledge acquisition. I am especially eager to delve into current policy and legal issues regarding mainstreaming and inclusion and the implications regarding like learner classrooms.

I intend to pursue a doctoral program that will allow me to further hone my skills as a special education instructor, clarify and further develop my concept of classroom operations for like learners and exceptional learners, and to contribute to education policy reform in the areas of classroom structure and operations, as well as assessing the learning styles of all students as a requirement, to determine and instruct them in the best way they learn. I would love to employ the use of the S-Factor Assessment to do so. It is my long-term goal to create a school for exceptional learners that provides an environment that acknowledges each student as a current and future scholar, where what is typically viewed as an adverse condition is seen as the very foundation on which to build on a student's innate talents and gifts. How's that for Interpersonal Effectiveness?!?

Self-Potency

I possess a strong self-potency that I developed early on in my childhood. While some would describe me as having an energetic personality others would definitely say that I possess an inner confidence, pervasive goodness, soul, quality of character, spirituality and courage (Taccarino pg. 5). I developed these qualities through my upbringing, the opportunities that were afforded me in school and in my personal life, and to some extent as a result of my ADHD condition.

Success Drive

The same can be said about my success drive. My parents helped to instill in me a strong work ethic. I have been working since the age of 12 and I can attest to the fact that hard work pays off in the end, whether it was illustrated through my successes or failures. Although, I would rather that parents and teachers help students to work smarter not harder, to achieve success. Dr. Taccarino states that children exhibit a strong success drive early in life but that our current schooling practices frustrate a child's emerging success drive by emphasizing test right answers in the context of instruction; providing passive, group based learning activities; and allowing children to experience premature peer competition and put downs. Encouraging and valuing trying, regardless of the immediate outcome of the effort, is essential in developing the success drive. Developing strong success tendencies should be the key assessment criteria in the schooling experience (pg. 6). One way to do this is to employ cooperative learning, collaborative learning, and peer and cross-age tutoring experiences (Fuchs, Fuchs, Mathes, & Simmons pg.152 – 178) in the classroom, which serve to lesson competitiveness in the classroom. I again I would also add that having students learn in a style best suited for them will also encourage sustained success in school. Employing the S-Factor

Assessment early on in a child's educational career, will help to determine the strength of their success drive and can provide solutions for further development or enrichment.

Other benefits of S-Factor Assessment

The utilization of the S-Factor Assessment can benefit schools in driving parental involvement. The assessment would be of good use in helping to identify ways in which parents can positively affect their children's learning. Providing feedback on areas for development can help both teachers and parents plan together the best course of action to undergird and promote successful academic achievement. Often times, parents do not know how to address their child's underachievement or how to enrich his/her strengthens. The S-Factor Assessment provides the perfect springboard for parents and teachers.

The S-Factor Assessment can also provide a foundation for school improvement among failing schools. By assessing students, pinpointing areas for development, and meeting students where they are at, can help in developing plans of action for improvement. To be sure, a school improves through the achievement of its students. Providing teachers, counselors, school psychologists, and parents with the information that best describes where a child is at and building from that point forward will help schools to make the AYP (average yearly progress) it seeks in becoming a high achieving school.

In conclusion, the S-Factor Assessment should be strongly considered as an alternative for assessing student academic and life success. It is a better indicator of student talent, skill, and measure of intelligence. It can help identify a student's true and accurate modality(ies) of learning and most expedient method for knowledge acquisition. Moreover, it helps parents to effectively help with their child's academic success by highlighting areas for improvement or enrichment. Lastly, in an era where our schools are failing students miserably, the S-Factor Assessment can help failing schools improve student outcomes by aiding in developing student educational plans that spur and drive student achievement.

REFERENCES

Gabrielle, A., and C. Montecinos. "Collaborating with a Skilled Peer: The Influence of Achievement Goals and Perceptions of Partners' Competence on the Participation and Learning of Low-Achieving Students." *The Journal of Experimental Education* 0 (2001): 0. Print.

Taccarino, J. "Success Readiness Development."

Taccarino, J., (2015). The Taccarino-Leonard S(Success)-Factor: *The Psychological Roots of Success. ,*Melbourne, Florida: *Motivational Press*

CHAPTER 6

THE CHALLENGE OF S-FACTOR TRANSFORMATION

By Megan Ambrose

In this chapter Megan Ambrose, a graduate student within the Counseling Program within the College of Education at DePaul University presents a case study analysis from the theoretical perspective of the S-Factor that explores bases for bringing about developmental transformation in a young student with multiple presenting problems.

MAYA CASE STUDY

Maya is an 8 year-old Hispanic female currently enrolled in 2nd grade in an urban public elementary school. Within her 2nd grade class she is considered more of a "trouble making student" behavior wise. She also has difficulty in most academic subjects, in particular reading and math. Behaviorally, Maya has had problems with her peer relationships and does not seem to respect the authority of her classroom teacher or aides.

Critical Health Factors

Based solely on appearance the only critical health factor Maya seems to exhibit is being slightly overweight. She has often stated that she does not like to "exercise" or play on the playground with her friends, which could be contributing to her weight gain. When asked to describe what she eats at home it consists of mainly fast food and frozen dinners due to the fact that her mother is currently working two jobs. At school she is fed a balanced diet as part of the Free and Reduced Lunch Program funded by the Federal government, however, she has described the lunches as unappetizing the majority of the time. Changing her eating habits at home could be of value as there may be a possible link between eating processed , high sugar foods and disruptive behavior.

Maya has never been diagnosed with Attention Deficit Hyperactive Disorder (ADHD), but often exhibits some of the key signs such as being easily distracted, disorganized, and forgetful.

Critical Environmental Factors and Family

Maya attends school in a low income Hispanic area. In fact, 99% of the school's population identify as Hispanic. Every student in the school qualifies for the Federal Free and Reduced Lunch Program. It is clear, however, that the faculty and staff go to great lengths to ensure that the children are in a safe and caring environment. Teachers create a trusting relationship between each of their students in order to ensure the students feel safe within their individual classroom.

Maya's home environment is one that is very different from the one she is exposed to at school. She has at least one younger brother who is currently 7 years old and attends the same school as Maya. He has been diagnosed with a severe form of ADHD and receives extra academic service support through the school. It is unknown whether she has any other siblings, but her relationship with her younger brother is often described by teachers as a very pleasant one. It was evident that she looks out for him both inside and outside of school. While working with Maya there were times when she seemed very upset regarding her parents 'relationship. After Maya was absent for several days in a row It was revealed that Maya's mother and father were in the middle of a complicated divorce and custody battle.

Educational Background

Maya's classroom is in a typical urban public elementary school. There are a total of 30 children in the classroom, one teacher, and no aides. Because of the student to teacher ratio it is difficult for the teacher to keep track of each of her students at all times. A traditional curriculum is utilized including mathematics, spelling, reading, science, and social studies. I worked with Maya in reading and mathematics as these were the subjects in which she was having the most difficulty. . When I began working with her she was reading and preforming mathematics at around a Kindergarten level. Maya was one of the students that seemed to be "slipping through the cracks" because the other 29 students in the class required the teacher's attention as well. Since she does not have a diagnosed behavior disorder or academic handicap she was missing out on additional services that I believe could have been of value for her.

As Maya has continued to move through school her confidence level has dropped significantly because of her slipping academic performance. She is old enough now to understand that she is behind the majority of her classmates and this has caused her to become hostile and unwilling to put in enough effort at times to help her to succeed. She often requires one-on-one time with the classroom teacher in order to ensure that all of her work has been done properly. Her classroom behavior has become a major part of her academic struggle as well. She often wanders around the classroom talking with friends in order to avoid the work she does not understand. Because of her task avoidance she is often portrayed as the "class clown" by her classmates and she appears comfortable in accepting that role.

Social Relationships

Maya is a very social 8 year old, which can be of great of value in elementary school. However she tends to take her social relationships more seriously than her academics. She often has trouble regulating her emotions and this has has caused some friction within her peer relationships. When Maya does not get her way she is more likely to either move on to a different friendship or cause a struggle. For example , if students are playing a game with Maya she always needs to be "in charge" of the game's rules and has a tendency to manipulate them in her favor.

Regarding her relationship with the main classroom teacher and the teacher aide , she would often try to bargain when discussing her school work. For example, if asked to do a certain number of math or reading questions, she would always try to have number of items reduced. She was also known for task avoidance when it came to more challenging elements of the academic curriculum. She would often be working on a computer when she was supposed to be reading or walking in the hallway when she was supposed to be in the classroom working.

Ethnic Background

As is the case with the majority of the students in her school, Maya identifies herself as a Hispanic female. Little is known about her family traditions relating to her ethnic background. It has been observed that she was able to obtain support from her extended family when needed. Since she has such a tight knit extended family I believe this will help Maya when she is experiencing difficulty regarding her immediate family and the divorce proceedings.

Maya's S-Factor

In the context of Maya's social and educational challenges, an S-Factor analysis may provide insight into how to better meet her academic needs.

By seeking to help Maya, her parents and her teachers should seek to obtain an accurate assessment of Maya's strengths and weaknesses regarding the six elements of the S-Factor. A plan for developing her S-Factor should then be formulated and implemented in association with her parents and teacher.

The following is a discussion of Maya's level of S-Factor development based upon the key elements of her S-Factor profile:

Internal Motivation and Self-Regulation

Maya currently has a very low level of internal motivation. She has made it clear that she is not motivated when it comes to academics unless there is an external reward in place. It has been difficult to gage her academic interests because she has been adamant in avoiding any task that required reading or mathematics. In order for Maya to be more successful it is essential that she become able to increase both her internal motivation and self-regulation. At her age it is essential that her teachers become aware of her lack of internal motivation and self-regulation so they are better prepared to assist her when it comes to discovering and developing her academic interests.

Self-Valuing

In Maya's case I would rate her self-valuing at a medium level. Her resilience and ability to "bounce back" after she experiences an unfortunate life event has continued to amaze me. Even in the midst of her parent's complicated divorce and custody battle Maya often continued to put her younger brother's needs before her own and came to school with a smile on her face.

Affective Effectiveness

Maya's behavior in the classroom clearly suggests a very low rating in this area.. She often has outbursts in class when she does not get her way. Her lack of affective effectiveness could be due to her young age, but I believe there is more going on that prevents her from exhibiting the social adaptability and impulse control that are necessary for her present and future success.

Interpersonal Effectiveness

This is a more difficult area to assess for Maya because she seems to enjoy her peer relationships, however her lack of impulse control and highly conflicting behavior often prevent her from doing so successfully. Other students have expressed that they have often chosen not to interact with Maya because of her "need for control" when working on an activity. I believe that once she is able to regulate both her temper and impulses she will be able to have very successful peer relationships.

Self-Potency

This is one area that I would rate Maya very high in due to her bubbly personality. She does have a big heart and often volunteers when the teacher has an errand or needs help at the projector. In order to further develop her self potency it appears very important to encourage her when she demonstrates self-initiative .

Success Drive

Since Maya is only 8 years old it is difficult to examine her success drive and assume that it will go unchanged throughout her life. At the present time, however, she appears to have a low success drive. She often looks for the easy way out and needs external rewards in order to complete most academic tasks. It seems clear clear that Maya needs a great deal of support and encouragement to help ignite her success drive.

Conclusion and Recommendations

Maya is an example of a young student who does not have a strong S-Factor at the present time. Although she has overcome certain obstacles such as having to deal with her parent's complicated divorce there are clearly some areas in her life that could benefit from outside assistance. My first recommendation would be to engage the classroom teacher in seeking to help mitigate the psychological effects of the emotional struggles she is experiencing at home. I think the teacher should create an individualized "reward system" for Maya as a first step in helping her to self-regulate her behavior.

A second recommendation for Maya is that she should receive individual counseling on a regular basis. I think this would give her a safe place to express her feelings and ideas without judgment. A counselor could also help Maya when it comes to developing her sense of emotional regulation and impulse control which she will need as she grows up. It is important for Maya to recognizes that she does have strengths and with the right support she can be a very successful individual.

In addition to the valuable recommendations for Maya that have been offered by Ms. Ambrose, I would like to suggest some additional bases for assisting Maya to achieve S-Factor transformation and a high level of success readiness.

1. *A formal S-Factor assessment using the " Taccarino-Lenard S(Success)-Factor Assessment for- Primary Schools" should be carried out to obtain a clear analysis of the strengths and weaknesses within the key elements of Maya's S-Factor.*

2. *If there are areas of significant weakness in her S-Factor profile it will be important to begin using "habituated intention" as a means of bringing about an S-Factor transformation in the case of Maya. It is very important to help Maya to understand how important it is for her to develop strengths in the areas where she*

has S-Factor s weakness in order to help her to become ready to succeed now and in the future. It would also be of great value to encourage her when she tries to build positive habits in areas where she presently has weaknesses.

3. *Helping Maya to further strengthen her internal motivation and self-regulation is crucial as this is the key S-Factor element that has a direct effect upon all of the other S-Factor elements. It is through the strengthening and use of her internal motivation that she will begin to develop the intention necessary for strengthening her other S-Factor tendencies. One of the key ways of building internal motivation is to encourage Maya to explore her interests and aptitudes in the hope that an interest becomes a passion in an area where she has a strong aptitude for development. If for example, Maya discovers an interest in dance and finds that she has an aptitude for performance in this area then we have found the golden key that could unlock a passion that could ignite her internal motivation. If she becomes passionate about wanting to become a dancer she will be open to stories that depict how highly accomplishes dancers have used the power of their strong S-Factors to help them to succeed. If she now sees a path to success as a dancer by following the models of those like her that did succeed, she is now ready to buy into the importance of S-Factor development by empowering her emerging self-potency and success drive. At this point she will now have the intent that will support the habit formations that will drive the process of "habitu-*

ated intention" in transforming and strengthening her overall S-Factor.

4. *An Internally motivated intent to change could now push Maya to strengthen her self-regulation in the service of building and consistently applying the habits that will help her to create strength within her S-Factor and bring her to a powerful readiness to succeed.*

CHAPTER 7

CASE PROFILES OF HIGH ACHIEVING AFRICAN AMERICAN MALES WITH STRONG S-FACTORS

By Sarah Royster

In this chapter Sarah Royster, a Chicago based school administrator, shares case study profiles of six high achieving African American men who share strong S-Factors and have clearly learned how to succeed. The case study analyses presented by Ms. Royster are very significant in showing the relationship between a strong S-Factor and other traits and characteristics that can provide a blueprint for success.

CASE PROFILES

What follows are sample case study profiles of six high achieving African American men who demonstrated S(Success) Factor strength based upon their scores on the assessment system developed by Dr. Taccarino and Dr. Leonard.

Each of these individuals grew up in different neighborhoods and in different eras: (a) northern urban integrated during the eighties, (b) northern urban integrated during the sixties, (c) northern urban segregated during the sixties (d) northern urban segregated during the eighties, (e) southern small town integrated during the eighties and (f) northern rural town integrated during the eighties. My goal in carrying out these case study analyses was to identify commonalities among these individuals that are associated with strong S-Factors as a possible new paradigm for helping African American males to discover a road to success through the strengthening of the key elements of their S-Factors as a basis for becoming psychologically ready to succeed.

Case Profile #1, Benjamin

Benjamin represents African American men who grew up during the eighties in a Midwest urban integrated community. He lived in a home with his father, mother and two sisters. Benjamin's parents were educators and placed a lot of emphasis on learning, so there is a possibility that Benjamin was born with some genetic factors that helped him to excel academically. His father was a Black Panther and his mother was actively involved in the civil rights movement. Their involvement with equal rights, made Benjamin acutely aware of challenges African Americans faced, but they also encouraged him to shoot for the moon in all of his endeavors and always dream big.

His early memories of the neighborhood were that it was predominately white and a place where he faced blatant racism on a regular basis. When he spoke of it, he paused and said "one day my older sister and I were walking to school and a white boy who attended our school stood on his porch and called us the N word and threw snowballs at us. My sister told me not to turn around, just keep walking. I'll never forget that day."

In school he was teased about his dark complexion, yet he leveled the playing field by excelling in advance courses and consistently maintained straight A's even in his honors courses. Many of his white peers and even a few white teachers could not understand how this little black boy was so intelligent. He recalls one of his teacher parent conferences where his teacher told his mother that he was arrogant. His mother asked his teacher if her son was meeting his academic expectations. When the teacher said yes, she asked the teacher to focus on educating her son and not judging his personality. Perhaps in retrospect what the teacher saw as arrogance, was Benjamin's assertion of self –valuing and self-potency in a system that systematically demeaned his value on the basis of racial bias.

Benjamin reported to me that the source of his emerging pattern of high achievement was stimulated when he was ten years old by his little league baseball coach. While playing a baseball game, his coach pulled him to the side and said "this is the championship we're playing in, I know you can help us win this game, do you believe you can help? If you don't believe in yourself and your outstanding athletic abilities, you won't perform according to your talents." Benjamin approached home plate and hit a double, which led his team to the championship. From an S-Factor standpoint the coach helped ignite his internal motivation by recognizing that he had a talent and encouraging him to develop it. Benjamin illustrates how African American men learn discipline and sportsmanship in extra curricula activities and how these events shape their desire to excel. In the case of Benjamin the coach's encouraging words became the catalyst that eventually led to the successes Benjamin later achieved in his long career as a major league baseball player. Sometimes we need someone to believe in us before we can fully believe in ourselves.

Benjamin also received a great deal of encouragement to succeed from his mother, who taught him to aim high and value education, and his father who taught him to love baseball and fishing. Mostly they valued him to the point that self-valuing became part of who he was. Once a person develops the S-Factor element of self-valuing , the easier it becomes to develop internal motivation and self-regulation. It is clear that Benjamin was learning how to succeed at an early age through the support and high expectancies communicated to him by his parents and coach. He was encouraged by both parents to love God, himself and others. His parents consistently told him that education was the key to success. They encouraged excellence and expected above average results. They taught Benjamin to believe in himself and help others along the way. From the models drawn from his parents he discovered at an early age the importance of learning how to succeed himself, but also helping others to learn how to succeed.

When I asked Benjamin to describe what or who put him on the road to success, he said, "I guess you can say it was my parents. My mother always encouraged me to stretch myself by taking me to the library and spending quality time helping me with my homework. My father loved to read and just watching him read everything he could get his hands on encouraged me to read. Today, I read about two books per week and I love to do crosswords. I find crosswords very challenging and beneficial for my vocabulary. I encourage everyone I know to read to children. My parents always told me that knowledge was power and I believe them, so I read as much as I can to gain more knowledge."

Benjamin excelled academically and athletically. He received a four-year academic scholarship to a top university in Missouri, where he graduated with honors. After completing his undergraduate career, he was drafted and received a professional baseball contract to play for the Philadelphia Phillies.

The cornerstone of Benjamin's success is his faith. He was raised in a God-fearing family and attended church regularly. Ultimately, his faith propelled him to a place where he simply believed that he could do anything he put his mind to with the help of the Lord. From a very early age, Benjamin learned the value of delaying satisfaction to achieve personal and professional success. His dominant S-Factor is internal motivation and he used it well to blend his success drive with his spiritual beliefs to find a basis for enduring and meaningful success. Benjamin truly learned how to succeed by developing strength in all the elements of the S-Factor and applying them in ways that allowed him to act upon his aptitudes and opportunities in a productive way.

At the time of this writing, Benjamin is thirty-one years old and married with two children. He is currently a business manager, entrepreneur, mentor and pursing his MBA in an accelerated graduate program for executives at the University of Chicago.

Case Profile #2, David

David represents African American men who grew up during the sixties in an integrated community on the Southeast side of Chicago. His community was integrated with African Americans and Jewish Americans. He learned early that he was different from most of his Jewish peers. He really didn't understand why he was treated differently at the grocery store or at school, but he knew there was a difference.

One of David's closest friends was Jewish, his name was Seth. One day while they were going to the store to purchase some candy, the store owner made David empty his pockets and accused him of stealing. David was angry and embarrassed. Although the owner did not find anything in his pockets, he told David never to return to his store. David was devastated and walked home in tears. He never told his parents about this episode, because he knew his father would have gone back to the store and exchanged more than a few words with the owner who had disrespected his oldest son.

David was raised in a two-parent home until his parents divorced when he was fourteen years old. When his father moved out, David's mother told him that he would have to step up and assume more responsibilities because he was the oldest of five children.

David excelled academically and had a strong desire to learn new and different things. However, while walking to the library, his friend offered him some marijuana. He smoked it, but said it did not affect him, because he didn't know how to inhale. Four years later, while attending a Boys Scout camp, four older white boys offered David and his younger friends speed and they used it. This was the beginning of a downward spiral into a life of drugs for David.

His mother struggled to protect her son from the apparent traps that were set before him by enrolling him in a high school for gifted students. Unfortunately, David was small in stature and was teased, so he became more occupied with fitting in, than excelling academically. His grades began to fall, so his mother sent him to live with his paternal grandparents.

His paternal grandparents were strict disciplinarians and demanded academic excellence. His grandfather owned a small business and required David to assist him with hard manual labor every weekend. His grandfather's goal was to teach him the value of an education so his grandson would not have labor as hard as he did to obtain a decent income. His grandfather had lived through some very difficult economic times and he wanted David to take his education seriously so he would be able to get a "good-job".

Despite the level of extended support he received,, David dropped out of high school and joined the Navy. It was there that he first experienced the joy of traveling and was exposed to alternative methods of coping. I asked David what was the key to his success? He said "there was a counselor who told him, no matter how many failures he had experienced, he saw something great in him". This is an another example, as was the case with Benjamin, of having someone believe in him and try to help him to become ready in believe in himself as the basis for forming the crucial S-Factor element of self-valuing. . The counselor challenged David to do something different, if he wanted different results. David was so moved by the counselor's words, he began to cry. He knew he did not want to continue using drugs and destroying his life, so he began to do things differently. This was an important moment in David's life as the encouragement he received from someone he respected was the key starting point for his commitment to the S-Factor elements of internal motivation and self –regulation.

His first step was to stop hanging out with his friends that abused drugs. The next step was to enroll in a class to get his GED. While pursuing his GED he knew he wanted to go to college. After he finished his tour of duty with the Navy, he immediately enrolled at Chicago State University. During this time, he became a member of a community church that taught him that he was "unconditionally loved by God, and all he had to do was have enough faith to believe that with God's help he could do anything." This was perhaps the spiritual basis for developing the key S-Factor trait of self-potency. David also learned the benefits of being patient and setting realistic goals. After years of hard work, David eventually obtained his bachelor's degree and began working in the educational arena to help young African American boys who were deemed "at risk".

David's strongest S-Factor element is his success drive. This uniquely coincides with his current aspirations to expand his small business. David has been clean from all substance abuse for over twenty years. David, at the time of this writing is married with two children and is the youth pastor at his church. He is also the CEO of his own transportation company. By any standard, David certainly learned how to transform and strengthen the elements of his S-Factor and found a way to succeed at a very high level.

Case Profile #3, Tony

Tony represents African American men who grew up during the seventies in the Midwest. Tony is an outgoing individual who loves a challenge. His mother raised Tony in a small rural town in Illinois. He is the oldest of three boys.

Tony learned early about the benefits of academic excellence. However, when his peers began to tease him for being so smart, he no longer wanted to be the brightest, he just wanted to be accepted.

Although Tony's parents were divorced, both parents were active and engaged in Tony's life. When they realized Tony's grades were dropping from straight A's to B's and C's. They immediately began to talk to Tony about what was going on in school, so they could assist him with the challenges he faced. They never changed their views on education and continued to weave a tapestry of love and support to ensure Tony that they were always there to assist him.

Tony's family lived in a rundown tenement. They were very poor. As the oldest male child, Tony supplemented the family income working odd jobs at the local grocery store. Although Tony worked very hard everyday after school and on weekends, he only made $50 per week.

From a very young age, work was important to Tony. He understood the value of hard work. He described himself as cautious and one who only made friends with other boys that were as ambitious as he. Overall, he was a good kid. He never started fights, but had to defend himself or his younger brothers on a regular basis.

Tony began to rebel against his father. He said "my father was a playboy and left my mother for a younger woman. I was bitter then, and I'm bitter now. My brothers and I had a very difficult time trying to fit in because my mother could not afford to purchase name brand tennis shoes or polo shirts."

I asked Tony who or what guided him to the road called success? He said, "that would have to be my mother. My mother provided a protective enclave for my family. Although they were poor, she never allowed them to lower their sights on the future. I remember her telling me, I was the smartest man she knew. She said I could do anything I put my mind to, because I was focused and had a gift for being cool under pressure. I always remembered her words and even when I wanted to loose my cool, I'd hear my mother's voice and immediately calmed down to portray an image of being cool under pressure." Again, this is another example of how important it is to be be valued by someone who is important in one's life. His mother's loving and consistent support certainly helped Tony to develop the essential S-Factor trait of self-valuing.

Tony also talked about a man named Mr. Johnson at his church who would take Tony to baseball games with his son James. Mr. Johnson would spend quality time with the boys telling stories about George Washington Carver and Harriett Tubman. He encouraged them to know their history and work harder than their teachers expected, if they wanted to do great things in life. Tony never forgot these words. This is an important example of how important it is to learn the lessons of success from the stories of those who have succeeded at the highest levels.

Tony graduated from elementary, high school and college with honors. Apparently the self –valuing he learned from his mother and the lessons in how to succeed that he learned from

Mr. Johnson were translated into his ability to develop internal motivation and a strong success drive. While in college Tony joined a fraternity where he established leadership skills and the ability to work well on a team. These were expressions of his emerging interpersonal effectiveness and self-potency. The leadership skills he developed taught him to persevere even when things did not go as smoothly as he expected. His fraternity became his extended family. The other men in the fraternity graduated and began their careers. They drove fancy cars and took luxurious vacations, while Tony continued to pursue his goal of becoming a dentist. Tony said "his ability to delay satisfaction prepared him to remain focused on his long term objective." This is a key element of his ability to strengthen his internal motivation and self-regulation as part of his process in developing a strong S-Factor and learning how to succeed.

Tony believes one of the most important things African American men need to learn is how to effectively use networking. He attends several conferences each year,to stay abreast of innovative solutions and to get to know people who can assist him with his goals and aspirations.

He completed his educational career with a DDS. Today, Tony is thirty-three years old and owns his own dental practice. Tony's strongest sub-factor is self potency. Currently, Tony is single and has a strong desire to get married and have children. Tony is currently an active member in his church and mentors young boys in his community.

Case Profile #4, Mark

Mark represents African American men who grew up during the seventies in the Midwest. Mark was raised by his single teenage mother. She gave him a double portion of her love so that he would not miss out because his father was not in his life.

His mother is an educator who told him that his only way out of his underrepresented community was through academic achievement. He remembers going to the library every afternoon after school, where his mother would sit with him while he completed his homework. While there she also encouraged him to read books about different animals, countries and cultures. Eventually, Mark developed a love for books and is an avid reader today.

Mark studied hard and excelled in mathematics and science. As an honor student, he attended classes outside of his community with a few other friends, who like he, were "gifted". Since most of these classes were taught by white teachers and attended by a majority of white students, the undercurrents of racism affected Mark, but this did not dissuade him. Mark said he always did his homework and knew most of the answers to the teacher's questions, even though he rarely got called on for the answer.

I asked Mark what or who led him to think big and aim for above average outcomes? He said, "my mother was my number one supporter and biggest encourager. She often put my needs ahead of her own and for that I am truly grateful. I can remember when my mother would not attend a monthly outing with her friends just to attend a school activity with me. She always said life is a game, play to win. Initially, I did not understand what she meant, but as I got older it became clear to me that I would encounter a lot of racism, but I could not allow that to deter me. I had to pursue my dreams at all costs."

Mark also talked about a white co-worker who encouraged Mark to pursue his graduate degree. He told Mark "you are too smart to settle for an average nine to five job, if you complete your masters degree you can really make some money." His co-workers words resonated in Mark's head. Although it took Mark three years to apply to graduate school, he gave a lot of the credit to his co-worker for encouraging him to think big.

Church was a very important part of Mark's life. His paternal grandfather was a minister and educated Mark about the benefits of reaping and sowing. He told Mark "to be careful because what you do will come back to you." As a child, Mark did not really understand what his grandfather was talking about, but he said these few words still govern Mark's behavior today. Mark said "I'm extremely conscience of others and work very hard to treat people like I want to be treated."

Mark's dominant sub-factor is self-regulation. Mark is a self-starter. He can define his goals and implement the necessary action plan to achieve his goals. He does not need a significant amount of external direction to remain focused on his goals. Mark said "there was a time when all of my friends were driving nice cars and wearing upscale clothes and I wanted to do the same, but I waited until I completed my graduate degree and paid cash for my car."

Mark completed his undergraduate career in Finance and ultimately completed his MBA from Loyola University with a major in Financial Derivatives. Today, Mark works full time as a futures bond broker and teaches young African American boys mathematics at an after-school program in the neighborhood he grew up in. Mark is currently thirty-one years old, married with one child.

Case Profile #5, Michael

Michael embodies African American men who were raised in the south in a segregated community during the eighties. His mother raised him with his two younger brothers. However, his extended family provided a much-needed support system in order for him to excel. Although his parents never married, his father was actively engaged in his life and assisted him during his transition from boyhood to manhood.

Michael spent most of his adolescence working. His father owned a small construction company and required Michael to assist him during summer breaks and weekends. This hard, manual labor convinced Michael that he did not want to pursue this type of work as an adult.

One summer, Michael was invited to attend Vacation Bible School by his friend John. Michael enjoyed the games and snacks they received, so he decided to become a member of John's church. Michael said "this experience laid a solid foundation for me to develop my faith. Even though I no longer live there, I still support the ministry because I learned how to believe in God and myself while attending that church."

Michael's mother was the driving force behind his desire to outperform his peers and even his brothers. Michael had to catch a bus to the other side of town to attend an integrated school with a much better curriculum than his community schoool offered. It was here that Michael learned the value of education and the determination to focus on long-term success. From his settings, both black and white, Michael learned skills that assist him today. From his experience with his white classmates, he learned how to be a part of a whole and how to get along with diverse people. From his African American setting, Michael learned that in the face of racism, good things would come in the long run if he remained focused and continue to work hard.

I asked Michael if there was a particular event or person who led him to success. He said, "I learned a lot from my mother about delaying satisfaction, which helped a lot, but I would have to say it was my baseball coach who made me think big." My coach taught me discipline and self-control. Although Michael's coach was white, his coach taught him that he could deal with life issues just like he played baseball. His coach taught him to compete with himself and always strive for the best. Michael said, his athletic scholarship to college is directly associated with his coach challenging him and encouraging him that it was an attainable goal.

Michael's dominant sub-factor is success-drive. Michael certainly has a strong work ethic and works even harder when failures mount. He is resilient, ambitious and self motivated.

Michael received a full athletic scholarship to a university in Alabama. He was drafted to play professional baseball in his second year of college, so he did not complete his college education. However, Michael said "when my baseball career is complete, I will return to college and earn my degree in Management." Today, Michael is a Major League baseball player. Michael is thirty-two years old, married and the father of two children.

Case Profile #6, Paul

Paul characterizes African American men who grew up during the sixties in a Midwest urban segregated neighborhood.

His parents never married yet his stepfather played a crucial role in his life. Paul is the oldest of three children. Paul called himself an underachiever during his childhood, yet he turned bitterness into achievement in his later years. His mother was a health care worker and his father was a self-employed carpenter. When he was twenty-nine years old he established a strong relationship with his biological father.

When Paul was fourteen years old he joined a neighborhood gang. He joined the gang because there used to be turf wars and that appealed to him. However, no one knew he was a gang member for a long time. He never participated in any violent activity andhe basically used the gang affiliation to learn how to shoot craps, win a few dollars and learn how to attract women.

Paul spent his adolescent years in a large urban community. He lived across the street from an active community center where he played softball, football or ran track each day. His first love was football. He mastered the art of playing football and continued to play in high school. His desire to aim high was set off when his football coach demanded excellence on the field and in the classroom.

His athletic ability gained him a football scholarship to a junior college. Paul was not satisfied, so he continued to pursue his dream of professional football and gained a starting position at a large university in Wisconsin. Unfortunately, the financial strain forced him to return home to obtain employment to provide basic food, clothes and shelter.

As with any successful African American man, this did not stop Paul. He earned a job at one of the largest marketing companies in America as a mailroom clerk. He established relationships with key people in the organization and continued to move up in the company. Several executives in the company became Paul's extended family.

One evening while Paul was working out a co-worker invited Paul to attend an annual men's conference with his church. Paul accepted the invitation and he has been going to this church for the past twelve years. Paul said "the pastor was so open and down to earth, he made me feel like I was accepted and understood. The relationships I've developed at church changed my life."

Corporate downsizing forced Paul to lose his job. Paul took the exam to become a fire fighter and passed. His dominant S-Factor element is internal motivation. Paul can postpone satisfaction which allows him to achieve tremendous successes despite the odds facing him.

When I asked Paul how he learned to achieve above average outcomes, he said, "my experiences taught me the moral and social values of hard work, perseverance and motivation. My family, coach and church members provided support and encouragement that caused me to forge ahead even when the path was not clear."

Paul is currently forty years old, married with two children. He is a a successful entrepreneur and coaches his son's football team.

Case Studies Overview

While assessing their journeys, it became important for me to identify the relationships between their family, community and adolescent settings. Do they all come from solid two parent homes? Did an extended family member help them navigate their way out of depressed communities? Did they experience an educational motivator that stimulated a different life course?

Although parental love and attention are directly related to determining what happens to a child, it is not necessary for a successful African American man to come from a two-parent home. Whatever the child-raising technique, ideally a child does better with loving, committed long-term attention from both parents. Parents are not just responsible for insulating a child from risk and warding off harm, parents make a large contribution to a child's success.

Each subject did benefit from an extended family. Their experiences were quite different but all of them said a coach, clergy, aunt, uncle, grandparent or co-worker played a vital role in their ability to create new ideas and move ahead even when the outcome was uncertain.

Another very important success indicator that I discovered was integrity. Successful African American men have a much higher probability to be open and honest in all personal and professional dealings. Kimbro (1997) revealed, African American men understand that character cannot be acquired, only earned.

The subjects in each of these case studies are all extremely disciplined. They understand that they must first master themselves before they can lead anyone else. A study by Dwyer (1993) revealed that if you're going to be successful ...in life, you must be able to define success clearly so that you'll recognize it when you achieve it.

REFERENCES

Dwyer, Don (1993). Target success. Holbrook, MA: Bob Adams, Inc.

Royster, S. (2004), _Success Tendencies Indicators for African American Men_, M.A. Thesis: Chicago: DePaul University

PART 3

Profiles of Individuals Who Have Used the Strengths of Their S-Factors to Achieve Greatness

This section of the book presents examples of the type of inspirational case studies that could and perhaps should be part of the content of school curriculums at various ages in providing students with models of S-Factor Strength that they can be studied and hopefully emulated in their own lives as bases for helping them to learn how to succeed . Obviously some aspects of the lives of these individuals have to be adapted with regard to content elements so that it is appropriate for the age levels of the students as bases for exploring how a strong S-Factor can be a powerful engine of success. Most of the individuals profiled in this section of the book succeeded at very high levels despite early failures, physical handicaps and psychological problems that those with weaker S-'factors might have been unable to overcome.

Also, we can learn much about the process of how Strong Factors can be developed by studying the lives and developmental experiences of those who have manifested very strong S-Factors and have succeeded at the highest levels. Case studies included in this book on Steve Jobs, Michael Jordan, Oprah, Hedy Lamarr, Jack Ma and the Kelly family that are important as resources for helping students to learn how to succeed were adapted from the book, " S(Success Factor, the Psychological Roots of Success." (Taccarino, et al, 2015) . The are other case studie in that book that can also be used by teachers and curriculum planners as resources in assisting students to learn how to succeed. These case studies include those who used their strong S-Factors to succeed and overcome obstacles such as: Stephen King, Frederick Douglas, Tom Brady, Derrick Rose, Vincent van Gogh, Ludwig Van Beethoven, Marie Curie, Robert Downey, jr., Adam Sandler and Lee Kuan Yew.

CHAPTER 8

WHAT JACK MA CAN TELL US ABOUT LEARNING HOW TO SUCCEED

By John Tacarino and John Leonard

This case study of Jack Ma, the father of E-Commerce in China, was co-authored by myself (John Taccarino), and John Leonard. This study brings out the ways in which Jack Ma learned how to succeed despite his humble origins and became one of the most influential persons in the world. This chapter was adapted from the book, " S(Success Factor, the Psychological Roots of Success." I would also like to extend my sincere thanks to Javed Rahman at MiirrorWalk for his great help in reaching out to Mr. Ma and his associate for the purposes of this chapter.

When a person such as Jack Ma is regarded as the Father of China's e-commerce industry, it is fascinating to understand that when he first went to Seattle as a young man in 1995 it was the first time he had even seen a computer. This was also his first encounter with the Internet. He immediately became intrigued by what the internet was and its great potential for becoming the basis for e-commerce.

Little in Jack's past had prepared him to become an eventual master of the Internet and e-commerce. Born in Hangzhou, a coastal city near Shanghai in 1964, he certainly did not come from a family of wealth, but he demonstrated self-potency in his early life by learning how to speak English and giving impromptu tours of the city to English-speaking visitors. His future became a bit bleak, however, when he failed the entrance examination at Hangzhou Normal University. He did not quit, however, but only tried harder. After passing the entrance examination, he went on to be elected the student chair of the college and received a bachelor's degree in English. After teaching English at Hangzhou Dianzi University, he left that job and started a translation service for companies doing business in China. It was his work as a translator that brought him to the United States in 1995 when he had his first encounter with the Internet. For Jack, it was like a fish encountering water for the first time. He learned to swim in the world of the Internet very quickly and soon had a web site in place for his translation business, *China Connections*, the first commercial web site in China. The site was launched with $2,000 in borrowed money. It would be nice to report that this $2,000 investment later was worth millions of dollars. Unfortunately, It did not as the company failed and Jack had to find a job with the Chinese Ministry of Foreign trade and Economic Cooperation. Jack Ma, however, never lost sight of the potential of e-commerce in China. He later pursued his dream by later going to California to seek early stage capital for the e-commerce company he envisioned, but he was consistently turned down by investors and few would even listen to his ideas. He knew he was right and they were wrong, so he persisted. He could have easily given up and gone back to China empty handed, but he did not. In 1999, he marked the coming of the new millennium by raising $60,000 to form a company called Alibaba. The company had the goal of connecting buyers with sellers on the Internet. Although the company was losing money in its initial years, Jack convinced a consortium of investors including Goldman Sachs to provide 25 million dollars of funding. The company finally started to show a profit in 2002 and since then Alibaba has diversified and became one of the largest and most profitable internet-based companies in the world. In 2009, he was named by Time Magazine as one of the world's most influential people. Amazingly, Jack went from being a person few Californian investors would even listen to in 1999, and in the space of a decade, to a person everyone in the world business community would listen to with close attention.

In 1995 the Internet was essentially non-existent in China and it took Jack Ma three and a half hours to connect to his first web site. But today there are more Internet users in China than anywhere else in the world. Much of this change was led by the efforts of Jack Ma to make the internet and e-commerce powerful parts of the life of China.

The following represents our analysis of how the superior strength of Jack Ma's S-factor helped him achieve what he has achieved:

Self- Valuing

Jack Ma has always believed he would succeed. He may not have been sure when he was young in what area he would succeed or how he would succeed, but he always believed that success would come to him. More than anything else, what allowed him to raise $2,000 to start his first web site in China was the confidence he had in his ability to succeed with the venture. Self confidence and the belief that one is worthy of success is just as necessary to the process of convincing others such as his friends and family to invest in one's dreams as the product, service or invention itself. It takes even more self -confidence and an even higher level of self-valuing to continue the quest for success when the dream crashes and burns. As Dr. Taccarino has pointed out, resilience and persistence are qualities that seem to be forged more from failure than success in the development of a strong S-Factor. Rather than quitting when he initially did not achieve the success he hoped for, Jack was resilient and became even more committed to succeed in his next venture. His level of self -valuing and his belief in his ability to succeed pushed him to seek new investors for the $60,000 he needed to launch Alibaba. While Alibaba failed to show a profit in its formative years, he did not sell his dream, but kept promoting and developing it until he achieved the major funding that allowed Alibaba to become not only profitable, but one of the most successful companies in the world.

Internal Motivation and Self-Regulation

Internal motivation and self-potency are clearly linked as S-Factor traits. Jack Ma was always a self- starter. No one pushed him to learn English when he was young. He wanted to learn it because he felt it would help him to succeed. He then used an early command of the English language to give tours of his city to English speaking visitors. He was self- motivated to converse with visitors in their own language so he could improve his own ability to use the language for business purposes. Later he used his internal motivation to set up a translation service for business based upon his English language skills. In other words, he was motivated from within to prepare himself to be able to act upon opportunities. When an opportunity arose such as the chance to establish the first commercial web site in China, he used his self-motivation to act upon that opportunity. If he had hesitated or waited even a few months, someone else would have taken his chance that later led to great success. This is an important success lesson for students regarding how important it is to seize an opportunity and not wait for another opportunity to succeed. Another lesson of success that can be learned from Jack Ma is how important it is to prepare for success and not take for granted the importance of searching for opportunities as bases for later success.

Beyond internal motivation, there is also the strength of his self-regulation within his S-Factor profile. I am sure there were more enjoyable pursuits he could have followed in his youth other than committing himself to learning such a contradictory language as English at a high level, but he disciplined himself to pursue his goal. I am also sure that when he first achieved great wealth, Jack Ma could have easily led a life of leisure and personal gratification, but his internal motivation and self-regulation pushed him to continue to build his company and be of great service to the people of his country.

Affective Effectiveness

Throughout his life and career, Jack Ma has clearly manifested the singular ability to read the feelings and emotions of others.

He has also been able to predict what feelings and emotions some new product or service will generate within a consumer population. Jack Ma had a feeling for and about the internet that was emotionally very powerful when he first encountered its operations in Seattle in 1995. It was not just reason or logic that made him commit to seeking to engage the Chinese people in the Internet. He read the emotional foundations of the Chinese people and he knew that the Internet was something they would gravitate to both rationally and emotionally. He could feel the attraction that the Internet held for himself and would hold for the Chinese population.

Also, the ability to generate enthusiasm for what he believed in and what he was selling is also a crucial element of the level of affective effectiveness that Jack Ma clearly manifested. Affective effectiveness is a key component of the type of business leadership that Jack Ma has provided. His loyalty to his vision and his passion for that vision is what it took for Jack Ma to start with little but an idea and then proceed to build an e-commerce empire.

It is easy to become depressed when one fails, but Jack Ma had the type of affective effectiveness that allowed him to rally his emotions and enthusiasm when his first e-commerce business did not succeed. Rather than allowing himself to wallow in doubt and despair, he used his strong affective effectiveness to try even harder to succeed in his next venture, the formation of Alibaba.

Interpersonal Effectiveness

Jack Ma has an extroverted personality that has thrived in his interactions with others. He is a natural leader who has used his affective effectiveness to generate enthusiasm in group settings and build strong relationships with others. He is clearly a master of the media in projecting an image and persona that is clearly larger than life in his country and in the world business community. He is a super-salesman who was able to convince savvy institutions such as Goldman Sachs to invest in his vision for Alibaba. Interpersonal effectiveness includes both being able to relate to people on a person-to-person level, but also being able to build enthusiasm and commitment from people on a large scale, media based level as well. Jack Ma has manifested a high level of interpersonal effectiveness in both these dimensions.

Self Potency

In many ways, Jack Ma is the embodiment of self potency. Jack has always acted upon opportunities and made things happen throughout his life. I have already cited an example of his self potency when he seized the opportunity to build an e-commerce empire in China. I understand that Jack Ma is stepping down as the CEO of Alibaba, but it is hard to imagine that at just over fifty years of age that Jack Ma will be selecting his rocking chair, or the Chinese version of a rocking chair, to spend his remaining years sitting on a porch and watching the sunset. My prognosis for Jack Ma is that he will use his self-potency to start something new that may become just as big or exciting as what he created for Alibaba. I recently read an article in Forbes Magazine that raised the question of who will become the next Jack Ma. Actually I think it will be Jack Ma. Innovators like Jack Ma have the capacity to reinvent themselves and to thrive on new opportunities and new ideas. I do not think in any way that we have heard the last of Jack Ma or what he could potentially create.

Success Drive

Jack Ma's dominant success drive is the product of his other S-Factor tendencies. He values himself and feels worthy of his success. This has helped legitimatize his need to succeed and give him the confidence to push forward in the face of any failure or challenge.

His internal motivation and self- regulation have both fueled and empowered his success drive. His interpersonal effectiveness and affective effectiveness have given him the means to realize the power of his success drive. Finally, his self -potency has provided the guidance system and focus that has allowed his success drive to provide outlets for his need to achieve.

In conclusion, although Jack Ma has already accomplished so much by harnessing his dominant S-Factor in ways that have brought great triumphs, there is so much more he can still achieve as individuals with S-Factors as strong as Mr. Ma's do not rest on past victories, but strive for more. Jack Ma certainly provides an interesting source of study for students who are seeking to learn how to succeed.

REFERENCES

Inside Story Behind Jack Ma and the Creation of the World's Biggest Online Marketplace. HarperCollins. ISBN 0-06-167219-X.

Popovic, Stevan "Jack Ma: The man leading the Chinese e-commerce market", *Hot Topics*, May 4, 2014.

"The 2009 TIME 100: Jack Ma". *TIME.com.* 30 April 2009. Retrieved "World's Best CEOs 2008". Barron's. March 24, 2008.

CHAPTER 9

LESSONS IN HOW TO SUCCEED FROM STUDYING THE LIFE OF OPRAH

By Esther Velazquez

This chapter presents a case study on Oprah Winfrey that discusses how a strong S-Factor helped Oprah Winfrey, one of the most successful women of the modern world, achieve what she has e achieved despite obstacles that could easily have defeated an individual with a weaker S-Factor despite her gifts and talents. This case study was written by Esther Velazquez and was adapted from a chapter that first appeared in the book "S(Success), the Psychological Roots of Success." (Taccarino, et al, 2015)

Oprah Winfrey experienced a tumultuous childhood and risky adolescence; however, I believe her strong S (Success)-Factor was the basis for her transformation and emergence as a businessperson, talk show host, actress and philanthropist. In this case study, I will discuss Dr. Taccarino's developmental theory of the S-Factor and reveal how Oprah exhibits the elements central to the theory.

INTERNAL MOTIVATION

One element of the S-Factor is internal motivation (Taccarino, n.d., p. 2). \ Oprah exhibited internal motivation since she was a young child. For example, she stated in an interview that she would watch her grandmother wash clothes in a large pot of boiling water ("The American Dream", 1991). Oprah states that at four years old she thought, " My life won't be like this, it will be better" ("The American Dream", 1991). Even at an early age, Oprah knew she would not be living in the humble conditions that she experienced in rural Kosciusko, Mississippi.

Taccarino (n.d.) argues, "to achieve, the child first has to know what it is he/she really wants to achieve and then be able to persist in the process of goal attainment" (p. 3). In fourth grade Oprah's teacher, Mrs. Duncan, was very influential in her life (Garson, 2004, p. 21). As a result, she wanted to become a teacher one day (Garson, 2004, p. 21). Oprah aspired to become a teacher, missionary and actress. Further, she has acted upon her dreams and did not just keep them in her mind. Oprah accomplished the dream to become a teacher through her show as well as teaching at Northwestern J.L. School of Management. At Northwestern, she and Stedman Graham co-taught "The Dynamics of Leadership"(Garson, 2004, p. 21).

Since her teen years, Oprah's dream was to become an actress ("America's Beloved", 1991). Even with her successful talk show, she kept this dream alive and acted upon it. Oprah was successful in her role as Sofia in the movie *The Color Purple*(1985). She was nominated for best supporting actress as well as for an Oscar for her role ("America's Beloved", para. 7). Today, she continues to act and is in the movie *The Butler*(2013) that topped the box office with 25 million in sales (Brown, 2013).Oprah did not give up on her many aspirations and continued to develop new goals and act upon them.

Self-Valuing

Oprah struggled with her self-value early in life due, in part, to her early experiences. Although her life with her grandmother was humble, it was safe. At the age of six, Oprah went to live with her mother, Vernita Lee, in Milwaukee (Garson, 2004, p. 13). Her life with her mother was challenging because of the poverty and lack of affection (Garson, 2004, p. 15-16). Oprah had two other half siblings (Patricia and Jonathan) and she always felt that Patricia was favored and prettier due to her lighter skin color (Garson, 2004, p. 16). Sadly, at the age of nine, Oprah was raped by her cousin and repeatedly sexually abused by other male relatives (Garson, 2004, p. 22). The abuse lasted for five years (Garson, 2004, p. 22).

Oprah states that she, "... was promiscuous and rebellious" ("America's Beloved", 1991) and at 14, she became pregnant (Garson, 2004, p. 29). Her premature son passed away a couple weeks after his birth (Garson, 2004, p. 29). Although Oprah tried to escape by running away and acting out, it was not until she went to live with her father, Vernon, that her life began to change for the better ("America's Beloved", 1991).

Taccarino states (n.d.), "the child needs a foundation of self-love before he/she is ready to compete academically on a basis other than fear" (p.3). I believe Oprah was able to value herself once she went to live with her father largely because he valued her. Oprah states she recalls her father saying, "You can't bring

C's in this house because you are not a C student. If you were a C student you could because I'm not trying to make you do or be anything that you can't be. But you are not a C student; you are an A student. So that's what we expect in this house" ("America's Beloved", 1991).Oprah achieved in school living under her father's strict rules. As an example Oprah, "became an honor student, winning prizes for oratory and dramatic recitation ("America's Beloved", para. 3).

Affective Effectiveness

Another element that is connected to self valuing is affective effectiveness. Affective Effectiveness is, "the ability to empathize and respond appropriately to emotional needs [and] is very important in areas where the individual has to work with and motivate others in order to become successful in goal accomplishment (Taccarino, n.d., p. 3). Oprah demonstrated a high level of affective effectiveness through her talk show and philanthropy. On the Oprah Winfrey show, she was very relatable, empathetic and the audience connected with her. This fact can be measured by her top rank as daytime talk show for 25 seasons (1986-2011) and her 48 Day-time Emmy Awards (Oprah. com, 2009).

Further, her empathy and motivation to help others is apparent from her philanthropic endeavors. Using her platform to help others, she created Oprah's Angel Network (1998) that asked viewers to contribute money to help others ("Philanthropist", 2011, p. 4). In 2007, Oprah funded 40 million to build a 7-12 grade school in Johannesburg- The Oprah Winfrey Leadership Academy for Girls-South Africa ("Philanthropist", 2011, p. 4).

Although Oprah suffered through child abuse, she was able to work on her feelings of guilt and responsibility ("America's Beloved", 1991), "... testified before the U.S. Senate Judiciary Committee..."and influenced President Bill Clinton to enact the "Oprah Bill" in 1993 ("Philanthropist", 2011, p.4). Oprah's affective effectiveness has contributed to her success. Her empathy towards others' suffering and need leads her to act, unite others to act and make a difference through large scale and united action.

Interpersonal Effectiveness

According to Taccarino (n.d.), "self-valuing, affective effectiveness and interpersonal effectiveness are heavily interrelated" (p. 4). Oprah has a strong element of interpersonal effectiveness. She is confident and articulate and is successful in illustrating her viewpoints. I believe Oprah's ability to be likeable and relatable to others has positively impacted her career and led to greater success. For example, her enthusiasm (affective effectiveness) for books led to her "Book Club" on the Oprah Winfrey show. As a result, Oprah has positively influenced viewers to read and book sales increased exponentially after being featured on the Oprah Winfrey show (Minzesheimer, 2011).

Self -Potency

In her early years, Oprah already demonstrated self potency through her preaching. Oprah asked her fourth grade teacher, Mrs. Duncan, to allow her to repeat the sermon from church ("America's Beloved", 1991). Although she was mocked by her peers, she did not waver because of her enthusiasm for reading. Today, she continues to exude self potency in all her endeavors. Self potency, "...also speaks to the person's ability to project a powerful, energetic personality (Taccarino, n.d., p. 5). The Oprah Winfrey Show has attracted millions of viewers across the world to be entertained and in many ways, educated by Oprah. Her self potency drew in faithful viewers day after day (42 million weekly) (Minzesheimer,2011). She discussed topics with such conviction and enthusiasm that the viewers were engaged and invested in Oprah and The Oprah Winfrey Show.

In addition, Oprah acts upon her convictions. She believes strongly in education and has granted scholarships through her charities (The Oprah Winfrey Foundation, The Oprah Winfrey Scholars Program and Oprah's Angel Network) ("Philanthropist", 2011, p. 4). Further, "Oprah's Angel Network has helped establish 60 schools in 13 countries..." ("Philanthropist", 2011, p. 4). She has become a teacher and currently has a show entitled Oprah's Life Class (OWN Network).

Success Drive

Children with a strong success drive, "...are ambitious, self motivated, resilient and have a strong need to succeed" (Taccarino, n.d., p. 5). Oprah exhibited a success drive early in life and it has not wavered despite negative life experiences and many failures. I agree with Taccarino (n.d.) that, "children often exhibit a strong success drive early in life, but it has to be nurtured and encouraged to flourish (p. 6). For example, I believe Oprah's success drive was encouraged by many along the way. For instance: her grandmother taught her how to read at an early age and encouraged her to recite bible verses in church; her father believed in her ability and intelligence and maintained high expectations for her academic career; her teacher Mrs. Duncan allowed her to preach to the class; and her college professor encouraged her to take the TV news position at the age of 19 ("America's Beloved", 1991).

Oprah is successful in many areas of her life and career. Nonetheless, she has also failed many times throughout her career. An example includes her production of the movie *Beloved* in 1998 (Garson, 2004, p. 18). Oprah was very committed to the film and invested her time, money and acting (Garson, 2004, p. 18). Nonetheless, the film took 10 years to make and flopped at the box office earning only one third (approximately $22.5 million) of the cost to generate the film (Garson, 2004, p. 18).

Overall, Oprah has made a profound impact on millions around the world. Her accomplishments are notable and historical. For example, Oprah is the first African American women to become a billionaire ("America's Beloved", para. 12) and "...the first women in history (1988) to own and produce (Harpo Productions, Inc.) her own talk show"("America's Beloved", para. 8).But she is not without failures. I believe her strong S-Factor elements have contributed to her being the Oprah Winfrey the world knows and many admire today. Her life story is proof that one's circumstances and failures do not determine future success. On the contrary, it is what one does in response to setbacks that determines one's future success. Becasue Oprah always wanted to be a teacher, she can offer valuable lessons in how to succeed for students who wish to emulate and learn from her successes.

REFERENCES

Brown, S. R. (2013, August 18). 'The Butler' earns $25 million at box office, finishing first ahead of 'Kick-Ass 2'. *New York Daily News*. Retrieved August 25, 2013, from http://www. nydailynews.com/entertainment/tv-movies/butler-finishes-box-office-article-1.1430236#ixzz2d0m5BUBZ

Garson, H. S. (2004). *Oprah Winfrey: A Biography*. Westport, CT: Greenwood Press.

Minzesheimer, B. (2011, May 22). How the 'Oprah Effect' changed publishing. *USA Today*. Retrieved August 25, 2013, from http://usatoday30.usatoday.com/life/books/news/2011-05-22-Oprah-Winfrey-Book-Club_n.htm

Oprah Winfrey Biography: America's Beloved Best Friend Retrieved from http://www.achievement.org/autodoc/page/win0bio-1

Oprah Winfrey's Official Biography. (May 17, 2011). In *Oprah. com*. Retrieved August 24, 2011 from http://www.oprah.com/pressroom/Oprah-Winfreys-Official-Biography

Taccarino, J. (n.d.).*Success Readiness Development*.

Winfrey, O. (Interviewee). (1991). [Video Interview]. Retrieved from Academy of Achievement Web site: http://www.achievement.org/autodoc/page/win0int-1

CHAPTER 10

STEVE JOBS AND HIS CREATIVE LESSONS ON HOW TO SUCCEED

By Meghan Huffman

This chapter was contributed b Meghan Huffman. It is adapted for an educational perpective from a chapter on Steve Jobs that she contributed to the book "S(Success) Factor, the Psychological Roots of Success." (Taccarino, et al, 2015). It draws insights into the persona of Steve Jobs who manifested a very strong S-Factor, but in a unique, creative and divergent way. To me this a very important case study from an educational perspective as Steve Jobs did not value traditional schooling as he believed it had failed him. I think it is very important for schooling at any level to address the developmental and educational needs of divergent thinkers such as Steve Jobs. As educators if we did not serve the educational needs of a man who changed the world, how can we respond more effectively to the needs of students who share the traits that caused Steve to question the value of his own schooling experience.

STEVEN PAUL JOBS (1955-2011)

"He touched every aspect of our lives--design, pop culture, technology, business--and created the very tools we use to express everything. For all this, and more, he was the man who invented tomorrow"

- Friscolanti, Kirby & Sorensen (2011)

Brief Background

Steven Paul "Steve" Jobs was born in San Francisco, California on February 24, 1955 to unmarried University of Wisconsin graduate students, Abdulfattah "John" Jandali and Joanne Carole Schieble. John and Joanne decided to give their son up for adoption to a couple having difficult conceiving, Paul and Clara Jobs. Overjoyed Paul and Clara named their son Steve, and the family moved to the Silicon Valley area.

In addition to learning how to work on electronics from Paul, his mechanic father. Steve grew up in the heart of cutting edge emerging technology in Silicon Valley. Ultimately, one of Steve's major influencers was his friend and business partner Steve Wozniak. Jobs and Wozniak developed their first computer together and officially started Apple, Inc. on April Fool's Day, 1976.

Steve Jobs went on to take these early influences and create revolutionary technology products. In so doing, he essentially transformed many of the tools of modern life.

Educational Background

Education was extremely important to Jobs' biological mother, Joanne Schieble. In fact, she almost did not sign the adoption papers because neither Paul nor Clara had a post-secondary degree. Because Paul and Clara promised Joanne that they would send Steve to college, she then she agreed to sign the adoption papers (Friscolanti, Kirby & Sorensen, 2011).

Although education was important to Steve's biological parents, interestingly enough Steve did not enjoy school. Starting at a young age, it was clear Steve was gifted. Steve had a naturally creative brain, but the structure of the traditional classroom experience that Steve experienced did not fit with creative needs and hands on learning style. As a way to rebel against what he perceived as the rigidity of his classroom, Steve would ignore his teachers and finds way to aggravate them by acting as a nuisance in the classroom. Steve's outlandish behavior appeared to be his way of communicating that classroom learning was not for him. Despite his setbacks in the classroom, there was no denying his brilliance (Friscolanti, Kirby & Sorensen, 2011).

Jobs' most notable educational accomplishments occurred outside the classroom. By the time he reached high school at Homestead High School in Cupertino, California, Jobs and his good friend Steve Wozniak were already underway innovating and developing electronic products. Later the duo would go on to establish the world-renowned Apple, Inc., but before this happened the two emerging entrepreneurs created their own phone hacking devices that turned out to be both illegal and unprofitable.

Paul and Clara Jobs kept their promise to Steve's biological mother Joanne and sent him to Reed College in Portland, Oregon to pursue his undergraduate degree. Similar to his experience in elementary and high school, the perceived narrow structure of the classroom was not conducive to Steve's learning style. Steve only lasted a semester at Reed College before dropping out in 1973. Apparently he spent the next year and a half experimenting with drugs. Steve claimed LSD helped him develop his creative abilities, specifically as it relates to beauty and art, which he experienced in a psychedelic state on the drug (Friscolanti, Kirby & Sorensen, 2011).

Although Steve dropped out of Reed College, he still attended a few lectures relating to calligraphy, which he loved. According to Friscolanti, Kirby and Sorensen (2011), these lectures and courses proved to be extremely impactful in the development of his skills for his later works when they write, "Years later, those calligraphy classes would inspire the fonts found on the first Macintosh desktop." Although formal education did not seem to work for Steve, he seemed to value learning, exploring and challenging himself as one of the greatest innovative thinkers of our time.

Work History

Unlike education, Steve Jobs really seemed to value his craftsmanship, or in other words his work. Steve modeled his father Paul's passion for working with his hands. When Steve was only six years old, his father Paul gave him his first set of tools and he taught him how to craft and fully make something with his hands. Steve continued this craftsmanship and extended it to working with electronic equipment and putting together "Heathkits". These radio and receiver devices took several hours and patience to put together. This practice instilled a value in Steve that he would carry with him in his own craftsmanship of Apple products (Friscolanti, Kirby & Sorensen, 2011).

Jobs' first business venture was with his good friend Steve Wozniak. The duo created phone hacking devices. This business endeavor earned them six thousand dollars; however, it was illegal so they had to shut it down. After this notable setback, Jobs went through a period without work where he experimented with drugs and was essentially homeless living on friends' couches. By 1974, Jobs decided to forego that lifestyle and enter into the workforce by first starting off at a video game start-up company called Atari. Jobs did not see a long-term career at Atari, so he began exploring electronics with his good friend Wozniak or "Woz" as Steve called him. Lucky for Steve, Woz was very talented in programming. Long before the two established Apple, Inc., Woz created the first personal computer. Woz' intentions behind creating this machinery was to showcase his skills to the other members in his computer club. Jobs, an innate businessman, had an entirely different perspective on the potential of this new type of machinery. Friscolanti, Kirby and Sorensen (2011) cite an interesting take on Jobs that was observed by Wozniak, "'He couldn't design a computer--he was never a designer or a programmer--but he could understand it well enough to understand what was good and what was bad.'"

Following the establishment of Apple, Inc. in the Jobs' family garage on April 4, 1976, the rest is history. Steve's business successes are truly remarkable. In 1977, Jobs and Wozniak unleashed a prototype of Apple II. Over the next three years, sales exploded from $2 million dollars in 1977 to $6 million dollars in 1981. In 1983, Apple joined the Fortune 500 and it was the youngest company to join the list. Friscolanti, Kirby and Sorensen (2011) describe Steve's overnight stardom when they write, "Steve Jobs--barely removed from being an LSD-dropping, anti-bathing fruitarian--was suddenly the rock star of personal computing."

Unfortunately, Apple's next round of products could not compete with IBM. In an effort to catch up with IBM's increasing sales, Apple came out with the Macintosh computer. Despite its creative style, the Macintosh could not reach IBM's level in sales. John Sculley, then CEO of Apple whom Jobs hired, began to phase Steve out, as he believed Jobs was hurting the brand.

Jobs left the company in 1985 and began a new hardware and software organization called NeXT, Inc. Additionally, Jobs jointly acquired Pixar Animation Studios with George Lucas. Pixar went on to become extremely successful, eventually earning $4 billion.

After setbacks with NeXT, Inc., Jobs returned to Apple as CEO in 1997. From there, Apple reinvented itself and sales propelled forward with the introduction of products, such as the iMac.

Jobs and Apple would continue on to create innovative products, such as the iPod, iTunes, Macbook Air and the iPhone. Jobs revolutionized modern technology, and hi created products that would transform human interaction forever ("Steve Jobs", The Biography.com website, retrieved Nov 6, 2014).

Personality traits and history of mental health

There is no denying Steve Jobs' business success and brilliance. However, with the success and brilliance came an intensive micromanaging tendency and radical mood swings. Steve, a natural workaholic and perfectionist, was known to be relentlessly critical. Employees would sometimes fear approaching him with work to review because they never knew what his mood would be.

Steve was stubbornly self-confident. Despite criticism about his management style, no one could deny Steve's ability to be convincing. When recruiting for a new CEO for Apple in 1983, Steve convinced the CEO of Pepsi John Sculley to join his team at Apple by stating, "Do you want to sell sugar water for the rest of your life? Or do you want to come change the world?" (as cited in Friscolanti, Kirby & Sorensen, 2011).

In order to seek to understand what we can learn from Steve Jobs regarding the process of learning how to succed, I would like to evaluate him the the perpective of the key elements of Taccarino's theory of the s-Factor.

Internal Motivation and Self-Regulation

Steve Jobs had a high level of internal motivation and self-regulation. Steve was not overly concerned with financial successes or fame, but rather he had a strong desire to create revolutionary products that changed the world. This behavior follows suit with Dr. Taccarino's S-Factor model when he writes, "They are able to persist in task accomplishment without specific or immediate external rewards or punishments" (p. 3). As a child, Steve's parents did not push him to stay in college when he dropped out. Rather, Steve had the liberty to make his own decisions. Steve's business endeavors were entirely a result of his internal motivation.

Despite criticism and doubts from his employees and the public, Steve was extremely persistent in carrying out his ideas. Steve valued perfectionism, and no one was going to stop him from ensuring a product was just right. These attributes are characteristics of an internally and self-regulated individual, as Dr. Taccarino states, "Persistence and resilience, key components of achievement, are primarily the products of internal motivation and self- regulation" (p. 3). There is no doubt Steve Jobs was internally motivated and had a high level of sel-regulation at least in the area of his work..

Self-Valuing

The second attribute of the S-Factor model deals with the topic of self-value. Dr. Taccarino elaborates on the benefits of being a self-valuing individual when he writes, "Self- valuing permits the individual to be resilient in dealing with failure and persistent in seeking to accomplish what the student feels truly worthy of accomplishing" (p. 4). As a child, Steve received love and support from his adoptive parents Paul and Clara. They made personal sacrifices in order for Steve to receive a quality education. Steve could have developed a low sense of self-worth since his biological parents put him up for adoption, but his adoptive parents' dedication to providing him with the best life possible helped support his sense of self-value. Steve's strong sense of self-value gave him the persistence to continue to work towards achieving his goals and ambitions, while also developing resilience when a venture of his failed.. Steve was never afraid to push limits and try new things, which ultimately made him successful.

Affective Effectiveness

According to Dr. Taccarino, affective effectiveness focuses on two areas. One area focuses on one's ability to be sensitive to and read another individual's emotions. The other area of affective effectiveness deals with creativity and divergent thinking (Taccarino, p. 4). Steve's affective effectiveness stemmed from the second area more than the first. It seems Steve had difficulty being sensitive and understanding others' emotions, as he was very self-involved. On the other hand, Steve was an extremely strong creative and divergent thinker. In his article, Dr. Taccarino writes, "Schooling too often delays the development and maturation of creativity in its students rather than sparking it" (p. 5). Given this concept, it makes sense why Steve struggled with classroom learning as it suppressed his creativity. This S-Factor attribute of affective effectiveness no doubt contributed to Steve's success through his innate ability to think creatively and divergently.

Interpersonal Effectiveness

Although interpersonal effectiveness is a critical component of the S-Factor theory, however this is not a strong area for Steve. In his article, Dr. Taccarino describes the importance of interpersonal effectiveness when he writes, "A person may have great ideas or a wonderful product to sell, but unless the individual can communicate the value of the idea or product to others in a socially effective way, success can always be just beyond the horizon" (p. 5). Steve obviously had great ideas and impressive products to sell, but oftentimes he did not take his employees' feedback into account. As a self-absorbed individual, Steve did not always interact effectively with his employees. In fact, a former Apple board member Arthur Rock once said about Steve, "Back then, he was uncontrollable. He got ideas in his head, and the hell with what anybody else wanted to do. Being a founder of the company, he went off and did them regardless of whether it ended up being good for the company" (Friscolanti, Kirby & Sorensen, 2011). Steve was so focused on his own vision that he often thought only he knew best. This mindset did not lend itself to interpersonal effectiveness with his empoyees , but he certainly connected with his customers as a super salesman for the products that he helped develop.

Self-Potency

Another component of the S-Factor is self-potency. Self-potency consists of an individual's internal motivation level and areas of interests, as well as the person's ability to project a strong, lively personality. "An individual's self-potency involves the level of energy, spontaneity, hope, joy of life, ambition, and excitement that the child brings to work and social interactions" (Taccarino, pg. 5). Steve Jobs was a self-potent individual. He had a high level of internal motivation, a wide variety of interests, and he maintained a powerful and energetic disposition. Even in the midst of battling cancer, he refused to stop working until he reached the point in his illness where he was doing his job ineffectively. Jobs thrived off of being spontaneous, ambitious and energetic, and this mindset showcased itself in his innovative work.

Success Drive

When Dr. Taccarino discusses success drive as it relates to the S-Factor theory, he emphasizes the importance of early education and its ability to either strengthen or deflate a student's success drive. "Schooling, on the other hand, often frustrates a child's emerging success drive by; emphasizing test important right answers in the context of instruction; providing passive, group based learning activities; and allowing the child to experience premature peer competition and put downs" (Taccarino, p. 7). Jobs' indifference towards typical schooling aligns with Taccarino's viewpoint. One might speculate Jobs' resistance towards school had a lot to do with feeling that his success drive was being suffocated by an overemphasis on things that did not concern him, such as test scores. For this reason and others, Jobs dropped out of school during his first semestir of college. On the other hand, Jobs' success drive was so strong that he wanted to learn on his own and to start working and innovating with his friend Steve Wozniak.

Finally, there is no denying the power of Steve Jobs' S-Factor. Over the course of his life and career. Steve Jobs used the strengths of his S-Factor as an engine of success. These success characteristics and behaviors were engrained in Steve. He would not let his health or anything else get in the way of his strong desire to succeed. He truly learned how to succeed in his own unique and creative way. The way in which he manifested his approach to success attainment may not work for everyone, but it certainly worked for him.

REFERENCES

Apple Info. (August 24, 2011). Letter from Steve Jobs [Press release]. Retrieved from "http://www.apple.com/pr/library/2011/08/24Letter-from-Steve-Jobs.html" http://www.apple.com/pr/library/2011/08/24Letter-from-Steve-Jobs.html

Cammeron, B (2011). "Steve Jobs Dies: A Timeline of His Health". Retrieved from "http://www.huffingtonpost.com/2011/10/05/st eve-jobs-health-timeline_n_997313.html" http://www.huffingtonpost.com/2011/10/05/steve-jobs-health-timeline_n_997313.html

Forbes 400 Richest Americans (Oct 8, 2011). Forbes. Archived from the original on 2011-10-08. Retrieved Nov 7, 2014.

Friscolanti, M., Kirby, J. & Sorensen, C. (2011). Steve Jobs. Maclean's, 124(41), 32-33. Retrieved from "http://web.b.ebscohost.com/ehost/detail/detail?sid=c9ea354a-6733-492a-8b1d-951a2d78d826%40sessionmgr113&vid=0&hid=11 6&bdata=JnNpdGU9ZWhvc3QtbGl2ZSZzY29wZT1zaXRl# db=bth&AN=66911559" http://web.b.ebscohost.com/ehost/detail/detail?sid=c9ea354a-6733-492a-8b1d-951a2d78d826%4 0sessionmgr113&vid=0&hid=116&bdata=JnNpdGU9ZWhvc3 QtbGl2ZSZzY29wZT1zaXRl#db=bth&AN=66911559

Isaacson, W. (2011). Steve Jobs. New York, NY: Simon and Schuster Paperbacks.

Steven Paul Jobs. (2014). The Biography.com website. Retrieved 05:26, Nov 6, 2014, from "http://www.biography.com/people/steve-jobs-9354805" http://www.biography.com/people/steve-jobs-9354805.

Szabo, L. (2013, July 2). Book raises alarms about alternative medicine. USA

Today. Retrieved from "http://www.usatoday.com/story/news/nation/2013/06/18/book-raises-alarms-about-alternative-medicine/2429385/" http://www.usatoday.com/story/news/nation/2013/06/18/book-raises-alarms-about-alternative-medicine/2429385/.

Taccarino, J. (n.d.). Success Readiness Development. Retrieved Nov 6, 2014 from "https://d2l.depaul.edu/d2l/le/content/311912/viewContent/2149278/View" https://d2l.depaul.edu/d2l/le/content/311912/viewContent/2149278/View.

CHAPTER 11

HOW HEDY LAMARR LEARNED HOW TO CHANGE THE WORLD

By Dr. Mara Leonard, Ph.D.

In this chapter Dr. Mara Leonard profiles how Hedy Keisler, a.k.a. Hedy Lamarr used the elements of her strong S-Factor to achieve a level of accomplishment few women or men have eve attained . She learned how to compete and win in some of the most dangerous games of life that have ever been played. As a success model for women she has much to offer regarding what she learned about success and how to achieve it. This chapter is adapted from the chapter on Hedy Lamarr that first appeared in the book "S(Success Factor, the Psychological Roots of Success." (Taccarino, et al, 2015)

Hedy Keisler, a.k.a. Hedy Lamarr led a life that was a life of paradoxes like some comic book super hero. She was Hedy Lamarr, a gorgeous, glamorous Hollywood movie star by day and Hedy Keisler a brilliant, mathematician and inventor by night. During her run as a movie star in the late 1930's through the 1950's she would spend her days putting in long hours on a movie set and on many nights go home to a small room in her Beverly Hills Mansion that was equipped with a drafting table and science reference books where she would work on the inventions and scientific theories that later would be the foundation for modern missile guidance systems, smart bombs, faxes, GPS, the wireless internet and cell phones. She may have also helped win World War II if she was the spy who gave Dr. Szilard the secrets of the Nazi nuclear bomb program that provided the evidence to convince President Franklin Roosevelt to launch an American nuclear bomb program.

She was posthumously inducted into the U.S. Inventors Hall of Fame in 2014 and her birthday is commemorated as inventors day in Switzerland, Germany and Austria. The irony of her inventions is that she never received any money for her patent that was the basis for world changing technologies. She gave her patent for wide spectrum frequency hopping to the Navy Department in the early 1940's as a contribution to the war effort. Rather than acknowledging her contribution, the Navy Department kept her invention a secret and asked her to sell war bonds for $25,000 thousand dollars a kiss. She certainly amply demonstrated her patriotism and willingness to kiss for Uncle Sam as she raised seventeen million dollars in war bond purchases. Although Hedy was certainly a good sport about this, to me, this was like asking Edison to go to Walmart and kiss every shopper who bought a light bulb.

. Anthony Loder, Hedy's only son, told my husband when they were working on a screenplay together about Hedy, that she could have become the wealthiest woman in the world if she had kept her patent and not given it to the Navy Department. In many ways this is an injustice as she had to rely on the exploitation of her beauty for the income she did obtain, rather than the rich fruits of her mind. After her beauty gave way to aging she was discarded by Hollywood in much the same manner in which she was discarded and exploited by the Navy Department. Despite winning awards for her scientific inventions in the latter part of her life, she was beset with money problems and died in a very modest home in central Florida in the year 2000. Because her theory of frequency hooping was so far ahead of its time, she never fully realized the great impact her invention would have upon daily life today.

Hedy Keisler was born in Vienna, Austria in 1914. Her father was a banker and her mother was a concert pianist. In her adolescence Hedy was a drama student and emerging actress. She came to public notice in a 1931 film titled *Ecstacy* that became an international scandal due to Hedy's full frontal nudity and a scene in which she graphically simulated an orgasm. Although she had a brilliant mathematical and scientific mind, she did not pursue formal education at a university, Instead, she essentially became a trophy wife. She married Friedrch Mandl, a munitions and military armaments manufacturer in 1933. He was one of the one of the wealthiest men in Austria and they lived together in an Austrian castle called Schloss Schwarzenau. Mandl used Hedy as an ornament to impress the political leaders and scientists he did business with in arms development and sales. Mussolini and Hitler were often guests at lavish parties at Schloss Schwarzenau. Mandl kept Hedy as a virtual prisoner in his enormous castle so the only contact she had with the outside world was when she accompanied him to scientific conferences or served as hostess at his weekend parties at Schloss Schwarzenau. It was during these parties where the armaments of the coming war were being discussed by the Nazi scientists who were developing them that Hedy's innate interest in and talent for scientific inquiry became stimulated. Hedy was very engaging and the scientists were very flattered that a woman of such great beauty would appear so interested in their work. If they had known they were talking with a woman who had one of the most brilliant scientific minds of the century and not the air head seductress from the film **Ecstacy** they assumed her to be, I am sure they would have been much more guarded in what they were telling her. She came to learn a great deal about the new radio guided torpedoes the German navy was developing in anticipation of the coming war. She quickly grasped that the inherent problem in using radio signals as a guidance system for torpedoes was that the frequency being used to transmit the signals could be easily jammed. Hedy became interested in seeking a solution to the problem. I am sure that the great scientists who patronized her and never solved the problem themselves would have been astonished to learn that Hedy herself would be the one to eventually solve the problem and give the solution to their adversaries.

In the documentary film *Calling Hedy Lamarr* that was narrated by her son Anthony Loder, it was brought out that Hedy may have been a spy for a power opposed to the rise of fascism in Germany and Italy. There could be great credence to this possibility. Through her conversations with important scientists working on the weapons of war for Mussolini and Hitler in the mid and late 1930's, Hedy certainly had access to information that could have been very important. Based upon a conversation my husband, Dr. Taccarino, had with a former neighbor of Hedy's in Florida, it is possible that Hedy may have been the unknown source that provided the key information regarding the status of and the elements employed in Germany's nuclear bomb program that provided the foundation for the efforts of Dr. Szilard and Dr. Einstein to convince President Roosevelt of the United States to launch the Manhattan Project. It was this project that produced the atomic bombs that ended World War II. If this was the case and Hedy was a later day Mata Hari, she may have been in very great danger when she escaped from Schloss Schwarzenau and fled to France in 1937. She was , however, willing to take risks for the good others and this is what made her self-potency so powerful.

Seeking refuge in the United States, Hedy boarded a ship bound for New York. On that ship she met Louis B. Mayer, the head of MGM, a major motion picture studio in the United States. Mayer soon changed her name to Hedy Lamarr and offered her a contract that subsequently placed her in several major productions. She went on to became one of the most popular movie stars of the time starring with such well known actors as Clark Gable, Charles Boyer , Jimmy Stewart and Spencer Tracy. Despite the demands of a movie career, Hedy continued to seek to find a solution to the problem of frequency jamming in torpedo guidance systems. She saw a possible area of discovery in a link between mathematics and music. Her mother had been a concert pianist and she was intrigued by how a piano produces music by varying musical notes. She then grasped the breakthrough concept that by varying radio frequencies jamming could be overcome. Working with her Beverly Hill neighbor, the composer George Antheiil , in seeking to apply her theory, they invented a punch card instrument similar to the operations of a player piano that used the 88 keys of piano to represent transmission frequencies. The devise could produce rapidly variable frequencies that would defy jamming. This theory of wide spectrum frequency hopping made possible the theoretical basis not only for military guidance systems, but eventually the cell phone, wi-fi, GPS, etc,

I believe Hedy 's S-Factor was extremely strong. I am sure its strength helped her to achieve what she achieved in very significant ways. What can we learn about the origins of success from someone like Hedy? I would now like to examine the roots of Hedy's success from the prism of the S-Factor.

Self-Valuing

As previously indicated, Hedy was born in 1914 as a child of wealth growing up in a well to do section of Vienna. Her father was the director of a leading bank in Vienna and her mother was a concert pianist. Hedy was educated in her youth by private tutors who helped her to learn -several languages. She later went to finishing school in Switzerland as a teenager. Essentially Hedy was prepared for a life as the wife of a wealthy man. Very little was expected of her other than being beautiful and gracious as a hostess. From the time Hedy reached adolescence it was clear, however, that she wanted more than this in life. She wanted her life to be special, worthy of living it.

Like so much of the persona of Hedy, there were paradoxical elements to her self –valuing, Because she was so loved by her father she felt worthy of her success. On the other hand, her mother was very critical of her as a child and I believe Hedy responded to her mother's criticism by seeking to prove to herself that her mother was wrong in her assessments of her. Hedy traveled a great deal with her parents and she often accompanied her father on long walks where he communicated his interest in and knowledge of technology by explaining to her how things like trains and ships worked. During her childhood Hedy was a bit overweight and her mother never saw her as being particularly attractive. She often compared Hedy to other young girls who her mother thought were far more attractive than her. Her mother loved her and devoted herself to shaping Hedy in the image she thought was appropriate for her, but she did not provide the type of unconditional affection that Hedy needed and received from her father. Rather, Hedy's mother was very strict with her and tended to focus on Hedy's faults and ignor or discredit her positives.

Hedy's self-valuing became as conditional as her mother 's way of loving her. She valued herself when she achieved at a high level and devalued herself when she experienced or perceived failure. Perhaps subconsciously she sought to satisfy her mother's conditions for judging her success or failure. On the other hand, her desire to invent was in many ways rooted in her father's interest in technology. She knew it would certainly please him if she achieved success as an inventor and she desperately wanted to please him. On the other hand, becoming recognized as a great beauty would satisfy her mother's condition for success. This pursuit of being recognized by the world as a great beauty was in many ways motivated by her mother's valuing of physical beauty. When she actually did become a movie star and was acclaimed by movie fans to be the most beautiful woman in the world, her conditional sense of self valuing was fed. On the other hand, when her beauty began to fade with age, she desperately sought to maintain it in a series of ultimately botched plastic surgeries that transformed her once great beauty into what she perceived as a mask of horror. This certainly threatened her sense of self- valuing as so much of her self-worth was based upon being viewed as beautiful. She eventually became a recluse later in life and would only have contact with those she knew via phone to avoid being seen.

I think toward the end of her life the recognition that she was finally receiving for her inventions helped her to gain a greater sense of self- valuing as she knew her father would have been very, very proud of her great success as a scientist as he valued this far more than physical beauty. In her final years she was still seeking invent new items such as improved traffic signals.

Internal Motivation and Self-Regulation

Despite her need for love, Hedy was certainly no one's puppet that could be manipulated first by her mother or later by her husbands. She definitely became her own person in a unique and original way. Although she was certainly influenced by her parents at both the conscious and unconscious levels, there was always an independence and individuality about Hedy that caused her to act upon life, not just react to what others said or believed. Hedy had an extremely high level of internal motivation and self-regulation. When she wanted something she was very direct and would go after it. She wanted to become an actress so she went to drama school and studied her art. She clearly manifested a form of habituated intent in seeking to improve her skills as an actress. In acting or later in inventing she was very persistent in seeking to put in the hard work and consistent effort necessary to succeed. The fact that she could spend highly focused hours at night working on her inventions after spending a demanding her days in a movie studio was certainly a clear testament to her capacity for self-regulation and internal motivation.

She was not motivated highly by things or rewards as money was always there for her in her early career and she often disposed of it quickly. She was clearly motivated from within as her success drive was fed by her curious mind. Whether she was in the moment experiencing success or failure, she was always resilient and always curious about and interested in the challenge of the next moment or the next day.

Affective Effectiveness

Hedy was very much in touch with her emotions and used her affective self as an engine for her self-motivation and self-potency. She also could effectively read the moods and feelings of others in ways that helped her to understand others and have a clear sense when to hold back or be assertive in seeking to achieve her goals or shape social situations to her benefit. Beyond just the allure of her beauty, it was her sensitivity to the feelings and moods of the German scientists she interacted with in the 1930's that made them comfortable with her and allowed her to gain access to their secrets. Although the military importance of her own work eventually far surpassed what she had learned from the German scientists at the parties she attended, it did provide the foundation for her scientific efforts.

Hedy was actually a very effective and talented actress despite the quality of the roles she was often given in her movies. In many ways it was her affective effectiveness that permitted her to feel and explore the emotions of the characters she was chosen to play. It is unfortunate that she turned down the two roles that would have placed her in the first echelon of the most successful actresses of all time. One was the role of Llsa in the movie **Casablanca.** The other, **Notorious,** was an even a closer echo of her own life in which she would have played a U.S. spy who becomes married to a Nazi collaborator and seeks to discover secret scientific information. Both of these films are now high on the list of the best pictures of all time. In retrospect it is truly a shame that she did not play Alicia Huberman in **Notorious** to help reward her for the very real contributions she made to the defeat of Naziism.

Interpersonal Effectiveness

Hedy displayed a very high level of interpersonal effectiveness throughout her life. She had a very engaging personality that quickly put people at ease in her presence. One component of her interpersonal effectiveness was her interest in what people believed and felt. This was one of the reasons it was so easy for her to gain the confidence of the German scientists from whom she gained so much information in ways that provided a foundation for her landmark scientific invention. She was well liked by both men and women as she was sincerely interested in the views and perspectives of others. Part of her interpersonal effectiveness was associated with her spontaneity, vivid sense of humor and the ability to make even common life events fun and interesting for others.

Self Potency

As one of the great inventors of the 20th Century, self potency was clearly the area of the S-Factor where she truly excelled. She was clearly an actor rather than a reactor. She was never the victim of circumstances as she was always looking for solutions and not excuses. When she was held as a virtual prisoner in Schloss Schwarzenau she did not allow herself to remain a victim of abuse, but she found a way to escape with all her jewels. She not only escaped the rise of Nazism in Europe, but may have played an important role in its defeat. When she wanted to become a movie star, she became a movie star at the highest level. When she was curious about the problem of frequency blocking in torpedo guidance systems, she continued to work on the problem until she found the answer. Even in her later years she still was trying to invent things and make things better for others.

Success Drive

Hedy was very demanding of herself and had a very strong need to achieve. The strength of her success drive propelled her to work hard and not give up even when she was experiencing disappointment or failure. She persisted on working on solving the problem of frequency blocking even when many thought it was a problem without a solution. She persisted when others could easily give up and she was resilient in the face of adversity and doubt. Essentially the strength of her success drive led her to become one of the most successful persons of her century.

In conclusion, Hedy was a model of success readiness. A strong S-Factor was part of who she was and what she became.

The strength of her S-Factor was not part of a transformation, but was inherent to whom she was. We can learn from her life in terms of how effectively she used the strength of her S-Factor as a foundation for all that she achieved in her life.

The first public recognition of Hedy's scientific accomplishments was achieved when she was given the Electronic Pioneers Foundation award in 1997. Mike Godwin, the spokesperson for the foundation, indicated that "the special award for Lamarr and Antheil is remarkable for other reasons besides its recognition of a woman whose contributions were thought to be solely in the field of entertainment. Partly this is because Lamarr and Antheil had hoped that the military applications of their invention would play a role in the defeat of Nazi Germany. Ironically this tool they developed to defend democracy half a century ago promises to extend democracy in the 21st century." (Press release from Electronic Frontier Foudation, 1997). To me the wording of the testimonial was very prophetic as it acknowledged what Hedy had accomplished and predicted the enormous future potential of her ideas for new technologies that subsequently brought so much to so many as cell phones, GPS, and wi-fi have so permeated our lives. It was wonderful that Hedy was still alive at that time to hear those words. In many ways, Hedy has provided lessons for how to succeed that are very important for female students to learn, particularly in the area of scientific invention

REFERENCES

(Press Release). Electronic Frontier Foundation. 11 March 1997.
"Hollywood star whose invention paved the way for Wi-Fi",
New Scientist, 8 December 2011

Hedy Lamarr, with Leo Guild and Cy Rice, *Ecstasy and Me: My
Life as a Woman*, New York: Bartholomew House, 1966.

"Calling Hedy Lamarr", *Mischief Films*, 2005

CHAPTER 12

MICHAEL JORDAN, THE MAN WHO LEARNED HOW TO SUCCEED BY LEARNING HOW TO DEFEAT FAILURE

By John Leonard

John Leonard contributed this chapter on Michael Jordan and what he has taught us regarding what we need to learn in order to succeed. This is an adaptation of the chapter John Leonard contributed to the book, "S-(Success Factor: the Psychological Roots of Success," (Taccarino, et al, 2015

To me the best test of the strength of a person's S-Factor is how that person responds to failure or the possibility of failure. Essentially *a person may fail, but he is only a failure if he has not given his best effort.* Michael Jordan passed that test at a higher level than anyone I can imagine in using a failure or the possibility of failure as a catalyst for igniting the full strength of his prodigious S-Factor to defeat failure and achieve exponential success.

In presenting this case study of Michael Jordan I would like to analyze how Michael Jordan used his extraordinarily strong S-Factor to achieve what he achieved. I will begin by applying the six core elements of the S-Factor to help us better understand how the S-Factor can function as such a powerful engine of success in the case of Michael Jordan.

Self-Valuing

I think that at some level Michael Jordan may have doubted his worthiness for success when he was younger. Self-valuing may have been a problem for him. As a result, he has throughout his life sought to prove his value by the weight of his accomplishments. A person who had a comfortable level of self-valuing would never have pushed himself so hard to prove his value to himself. His defeats or even possibilities of defeat, have always ignited his success drive in ways that pushed him to the highest levels of success.

When people talk about the great game winning shots that he made, Michael talks about the potentially game winning shots that he missed. He likely remembers every one of those missed shots, because each one he missed caused him to try harder, focus more and compete harder to succeed the next time he had the opportunity to take the big shot.

Another problem that Michael Jordan has had regarding self-valuing is that he did not succeed in the sport he really valued the most. It is likely that he wanted to be a professional baseball player more than a professional basketball player. His ultimate basis for self valuing may have been becoming successful as a major league baseball player. Perhaps in some way the awards he achieved in basketball in some way mocked his real desire to become a major league baseball player. Why else would he he have given up basketball at the very pinnacle of his career, to decide to try to become a major league baseball player in his early thirties. I think its possible that Jordan, perhaps subconsciously, was trying to ultimately prove to himself his self-value by pursuing success in the sport he valued the most. If he succeeded in baseball he could clearly value himself upon the conditions for self-valuing that he could fully accept. It is in many ways very sad that the baseball strike of 1995-1996 ended his dream of making it to the major leagues. Jordan effectively applied habituated intention to the process of developing the skills and performance level that could take him to the major leagues of baseball. There is no question he was getting better and may have made it to the big league roster of the Chicago White Sox on his own merits if the baseball strike did not halt his progress. I am sure it must have been a melancholy moment for him when the plane taking him back to Chicago to rejoin the Bulls tipped its wings as it flew over the White Sox Spring training facility in Sarasota.

Michael Jordan's sense of self-valuing was certainly tested when he returned from baseball and experienced a clear taste of failure when he was humiliated in a basketball playoff game when a ball was stolen from him in a play by Nick Anderson that led to an Orlando Magic victory. The Bulls lost the series and there was talk that Air Jordan had been grounded and that he could no longer play at his former level of greatness. Jordan responded to the challenge by working tremendously hard the next summer to not only regain, but improve his original game. He then not only led the Bulls to the NBA Championship, but helped them set the record for the most games won by an NBA team in the history of the league.

Internal Motivation and Self-Regulation

I can see why Dr. Taccarino contends that the core elements of the S-Factor are connected as each is influenced by the others. Michael Jordan learned that a key basis for overcoming self-doubt and finding a way to succeed was developing the habit of internal motivation and self-regulation. He learned how important it was to find the motivation to succeed within himself and regulate his behavior to give himself the push and consistency to do the hard work necessary to put himself in a position to succeed. In Jordan's case a positive *failure response* seems to operate in conjunction with the great strength of his S-Factor. At times he seemed to need a real or perceived failure to fully ignite his **Success Drive.** When Jordan's success drive has been threatened by actual failure or the possibility of failure he has responded by revving up his already high level of **internal motivation and self-regulat**ion

When Jordan was cut from his varsity high school basketball team and placed on the Junior Varsity Squad, he did not quit or pout. He used his internal motivation and self-regulation to work hard at developing his body and skills as a basketball player to prove his coach wrong in cutting him. Although his old coach has become almost a comic figure for having cut the greatest player in the history of the game from his team, the reality was that Jordan was not the greatest player in the history of the game at the time he was cut. However, by the time Jordan's high school career had ended. he not only had made the varsity team, but became a Mac Donald's All American.

When Jordan subsequently earned a basketball scholarship at the University of North Carolina some observers thought he could be a good college player, but not great. Jordan perhaps used that assessment to stoke his very strong level of internal motivation and self-regulation and push himself to further improve his performance as a basketball player. By the end of his first year he disproved any doubts regarding his potential greatness as a college player by hitting the shot that won the National Championship for the University of North Carolina. Making that shot was crucial for Jordan regarding its effect upon his sense of self-valuing. He knew that he could have passed up the shot or taken it and missed it, but he made it. From that point on Michael was able to put any lingering fears of failure to rest and develop the level of self-valuing to take those kind of game deciding shots without doubt or fear. From then on he knew that if the game was on the line, he should take the last shot if he was open or even a little bit open. A winner had fully learned how to win.

The strength of Jordan's internal motivation and self-regulation had given him the confidence to take game deciding shots because he had worked hard enough and prepared long enough to take them. In his final year at the University of North Carolina he was named the National College Player of the Year. He had conquered the world of college basketball and was now looking for new worlds to conquer.

Affective Effectiveness

Jordan may have been disappointed when two other players were picked ahead of him in the NBA draft. Many experts thought that he had a great college game, but it might not translate to the pro level. Most of the experts seemed to think that he could be a good pro player and might some day make the All Star Team, but no one seemed to think that he could be a future superstar except Michael himself. Michael tapped into his affective effectiveness to create the determination and focus to adapt his game to the pro style and by the end of his first month of play as a pro he was on the cover of Sports Illustrated and being hailed as an emerging superstar.

There was always an affective, emotional part of Michael's game that was as strong as the physical part of his game. Jordan knew how to trigger his own emotional responses, such as when he felt disrespected by others, to ignite the other core elements of his S-Factor to push himself to succeed. When Jordan appeared in the All Star Game in his first year as a pro several established players led by Isaiah Thomas, perhaps jealous of Jordan's quick ascent to immense fan popularity, tried to freeze him out by keeping the ball away from him to prevent him from dominating the game with his talent. For many years Thomas was Jordan's nemesis as his team, the Detroit Pistons ,were the closed door to any championship hopes for the Bulls.

In pro basketball trash talking is a way of establishing emotional dominance over another player. Using his high level of affective effectiveness Jordan quickly learned how to read the emotional profile of other players and use their vulnerabilities and weaknesses to psychologically distract them on the court and win the battles of emotional dominance. When Michael Jordan and the Chicago Bulls defeated the Detroit Pistons in the Conference Championship Series in 1990, they had not only won the physical battle, but the battle of affective dominance as well. Isaiah Thomas refused to shake Jordan's hand after the final game in a defiant symbol that reflected the affective part of their battle.

A similar battle for dominance played out in the NBA Championship series that year. Magic Johnson had long been considered the best active player in the NBA and Jordan was his challenger. In many ways the championship series was being framed as being like a Heavyweight Championship bout between Jordan and Johnson. If that's what it was, Jordan clearly won by a knockout as the Bulls went on to win their first NBA Championship and Jordan had clearly become the new Alpha male of the NBA.

Interpersonal Effectiveness

Michael Jordan has manifested a very high level of **interpersonal effectivess** in many aspect of his life and he has used that effectiveness as a core element of his bases for success. Being a tremendous leader and getting the most out his teammates in pressure situations has been clearly chronicled throughout his career. Certainly his ability to channel and blend his talents with those of his teammates was one of the key reasons why the Bulls won six NBA Championships.

However, the area where I see the greatest manifestation of his interpersonal effectiveness was his ability to connect with not only his team's fans , but people throughout the world. The world public saw something human, genuine and approachable about Michael that made them want to know him and buy the products he was endorsing. They wanted to wear his uniform and bounce around in Air Jordan shoes. People just liked Mike and they still do. Although years have passed since he last retired, he is still in demand as an endorser and his shoes and shirts are still among the best sellers throughout the world. There have been other great athletes in sports history, but none more liked than Mike.

Michael also showed great interpersonal effectiveness when he demonstrated so clearly that he felt a responsibility to his fans. Even when he was ill, injured or needed to rest for the playoffs, Jordan showed up. He did not take games off when his fans, often the fans in other cities, had paid maybe a day's wages to have them and their children get a chance to see him play.

Self-Potency

When Michael Jordan came into the NBA in 1984 it certainly was not the NBA of today. Not long before his coming to the NBA, the finals were being telecast in late night tape delays so the games would not interfere with the viewers desire to watch *I love Lucy* or *All in the Family*. Michael Jordan reinvented star power and made the NBA one of the most popular sports leagues in the world. He saw an opportunity to merchandise himself as a brand based upon his charisma and spectacular way of playing the game of basketball. That brand has become so successful and so enduring that Michael has become the first athlete in the history of sports to become a billionaire (*Forbes, 2015*). In many ways he has become one of the great business entrepreneurs of modern history. He saw an opportunity and acted upon it. That is self-potency.

Success Drive

For a lot of people Jordan made it seem all right to fail as long as one put in the effort to try to succeed. He gave us the hope that failing is just the next thing before success. As mentioned previously, it was as if he needed a failure or the possibility of imminent failure in order to give him the push to succeed.

One of the best examples of the strength of Jordan's success drive and his ability to meet the challenge of potential failure was when the Bulls were going for their sixth NBA Championship against the Utah Jazz in 1998. He was poisoned by a pizza in Utah and appeared to be nearly clinically dead as he willed himself to play anyway. In the key sixth game against the Jazz he was missing the vast majority of his shots as the team as a whole looked to be on the verge of collapse as the Jazz held the lead as the game was drawing to a close. The Jazz fans were cheering ecstatically as they knew their team would have defined momentum if there would be a deciding game seven in Chicago. In the closing seconds Karl Malone, the man who had beaten Jordan to win the league's Most Valuable Player Award that year, had the ball near the Bull's basket for the game icing shot. Defeat did not seem just possible for Jordan and the Bulls, but inevitable. Suddenly Jordan smashed the ball out of Karl Malone's hands, dribbled down the court with time about to expire and hit the shot that won the championship for the Bulls. Jordan retired again and this time it seemed fine as he could now rest upon his widely recognized laurels as the greatest player of all time in a perfect ending for a perfect career.

So what did Jordan do? Two years later he came back as a player with the Washington Generals, I mean Washington Wizards, to provide much less than a perfect ending to his career. Why did he have to come back to basketball at that point? Maybe he should have tried to prove he could play lacrosse instead. As a Bulls fan I would prefer just to have amnesia regarding what happened after he left the Bulls.

In any case, as a Bulls fan when I was very young and just getting a sense of sports and the successes and failures of completion, it was wonderful to have Michael Jordan on our side in knowing that he would inevitably rise from the brink of failure and slay the dragon of potential defeat. He certainly helped me, and others of my age, to learn not to fear failure or the possibility of failure, but to focus on what we have to do to succeed. He can also be an important model for helping students to learn how to succeed in sports, business and in life.

REFERENCES

Morris, Mike. "The Legend: A Highlight-Reel History of the NBA's Greatest Player". *Michael Jordan: The Ultimate Career Tribute*. Bannockburn, IL: H&S Media, 1999.

Smith, Sam, " The Jordan Rules", New York: Simon and Schuster, 1992

Smith, Sam, "The Second Coming: The Strange Odyssey of Michael Jordan from Courtside to Home Plate and Back Again." New York: HarperCollins, 1995

Taccarino, John, et al. "S(Success Factor. The Psychological Roots of Success."Melbourne, Florida: Motivational Press, 2015

CHAPTER 13

HOW THE KELLY FAMILY LEARNED HOW TO SUCCEED

By John Taccarino

The lessons of success can not only be learned from the study of successful individuals, but from successful families as well. This is particularly true when the family creates a culture of success that is passed on from generation to generation. The Kelly family is an excellent example of how a particular family created a culture of success based upon the development and nurturance of strong S-Factors within the members of this family. Next to the Kennedy's and possibly surpassing them in some areas, the Kelly's are one of the most successful Irish-American families in the U.S. and the impact of the lives of its members certainly went beyond the boundaries of Ireland and the United States. This chapter was written by John Taccarino.

The first generation of Kelly's, Mary and Michael, came to America in poverty in the late 1860's, but their descendants won a great fortune, a Pulitzer Prize, an Oscar, 3 Olympic gold medals and a royal crown for Princess Grace of Monaco. In this chapter I will seek to explain how the Kelly's learned how to succeed by creating a culture of shared S-Factor strength that was passed on through generations despite obstacles and often significant tragedies. The success the Kelly's achieved as a family was also firmly ground in the moral and ethical expectancies defined for her family by Mary Kelly. Mary was very much the moral compass for honesty and ethical behavior that has served the Kelly family as a foundation for the actions and activities of its individual members. The Kelly's learned how to succeed, but within the context and framework of a very clearly identified moral and ethical compass. Success that was not consistent with ethics and morality had no meaning for Mary Kelly and she clearly communicated that principle to her children.

John Henry and Mary Kelly

As I have indicated, Mary Costello Kelly and John Henry Kelly left Ireland in the late 1860's, fleeing the poverty and despair that followed from half the population of Ireland either dying from famine or emigrating due to extreme poverty and political oppression. What was so unique about Mary and John Henry Kelly that allowed them to found a family that achieved so much success when their origins were so humble? To me Mary and John Henry and Mary Kelly both had very strong S-Factors and they instilled its demands and tendencies in their eight children. Things were never easy for Mary and John Henry when they married upon coming to America. They settled and began their family in Philadelphia. They lived most of their lives in a small row house in a dreary and tough part of North Philadelphia.

When their family was growing up John Henry was often out of work due to lay offs at the textile mill where he labored. Mary took in washing to help make ends meet. On the other hand, they laughed a lot, supported each other and valued literature and sports. Mary made the power of words very important to her children as she often held a baby in one arm and a skittle in another as she recited the works of Shakespeare to her children. John Henry valued literature as well and could recite an entire book from memory. Their home was a home of great conversation and the challenge of ideas and athletic competition. Mary believed in her eight children and their potentials to succeed. She demanded their best in all that they did. John Henry set an example for his children when he took a job others were afraid to take because he wanted more for his family. It was a job as a conductor on a horse drawn trolley that made its way from center city Philadelphia to the outlying village of Manayunk. No one wanted the job because the former conductors were constantly being beaten up by the rowdy patrons who were exiting the many taverns along its route. John Henry, a powerful man and boxer of note, soon established order through the force of his fists. He had earned a secure job for the first time and life became a bit easier for the Kelly's. The children of the family learned from their father that life could be hard and it took great effort and courage to succeed. All of John Henry's and Mary's children demonstrated the qualities of strong S-Factors that were instilled by the culture of their family.. To me the key thing about the Kelly's was that they would never quit on their dreams and would never give up despite the many failures, injustices, disappointments and tragedies they experienced in pursuing success. .They all appeared to exhibit a self valuing that allowed them to feel worthy of success and they persisted in seeking their goals even when they experienced defeat or rejection. Defeats or rejections only seemed to make them try harder.

Walter and the first Grace Kelly

The first of the Kelly children to experience a high level of success was the oldest, Walter. He certainly displayed self potency, a strong success drive, internal motivation and self-regulation when he broke into vaudeville and took the initiative to develop a highly acclaimed act called *The Virginia Judge* that was a favorite of American Presidents in the 1890;s and the beginning years of the 20th Century.. Walter used his earnings to help his younger siblings to pursue their dreams of success on the stage or through sports. There has always been a mixture of tragedy and triumph as the children of Mary and John Henry followed their dreams of success. Grace, their only daughter, was a promising young actress who died tragically while seeking to establish herself as a working professional.

George Kelly

George Kelly entered vaudeville in the path of his brother Walter,, but he wanted more. He wanted to write great plays, but his early works were ignored because he lacked formal education. He saw this as an injustice as he thought his works should be judged on their merits alone. Rather than quitting or going back to vaudeville, he worked even harder to improve his skills as an author. He eventually won a Pulitzer Prize for Drama and became one of the leading playwrights of the 1920's . Six of his plays eventually became motion pictures. Like his brother

Walter who had helped him, he sought to share his success by helping members of his family shape and pursue their own dreams of success. He subsequently gave a role in one of his plays to his twelve year old niece, Grace, who at that time was quiet, shy and lacked confidence in herself. It was her first appearance on the stage, but it ignited a dream of success in acting that eventually led to an attainment of an Oscar .and a place as one of the great stars in motion picture history.

John B. Kelly

The youngest of the Kelly children was John B. Kelly. He was a gifted athlete who had a great deal of potential for success in sports, but potential does not often result in success if the person has a weak S-Factor. In the case of John B. Kelly he had a very strong S-Factor and he certainly needed it to overcome the obstacles that could have easily defeated a person with a weaker S-Factor. Rowing was John B. Kelly's sport of choice as it was a very popular in Philadelphia in the early years of the 20th Century. John B. dreamed of becoming the greatest oarsman in the history of the sport when he put in long hours during his teen years training for his future by rowing on the Schuylkill River. That dream seemed possible when he first won the U.S. Single Scull championship while still in his early twenties. Unfortunately he did not seize the moment to take on the best of the best by applying for entry to the Diamond Sculls Competition at the Henley Regatta in England, the most prominent race in rowing. At the time he believed that he needed more experience to develop his skills and felt he could enter the competition the following year. Unfortunately the same opportunity did not present itself during following year as the Henley Regatta was cancelled not just for that year, but for the five years of the duration of World War I. Although John B. continued to win U.S. Championships he was never able to prove himself at the international level of competition and realize his dream of becoming the greatest oarsman in the history of the sport. The chance of proving himself to be the best in his sport became less and less possible as the war continued and he grew older. Things became even darker for his dream when he was drafted for service with the American Expeditionary Force and sent France in 1917. Although some might call his dream a pipe dream at this point, John B. spent much of his spare time planning strategies for the races he hoped would still come. To keep in shape John B. turned to his other sport, boxing, when it was impossible to row. He was so talented as a boxer that he made it to the semi-finals of the Allied Forces heavyweight boxing competition. His opponent in the semi-finals was to be Gene Tunney, the future heavyweight champion of the world. Many thought he could beat Tunney and go on to a professional career, but tragedy struck when John B. broke his ankle in training and was never the same as a boxer. He would not face Tunney and his chance of becoming the heavyweight champion of the world was over. Rather than being brought down by this tragedy, Kelly displayed the strength of his S-Factor by renewing his commitment to rowing. Kelly told his friends that although his injury had cost him his foot speed as a boxer, it had no effect on his rowing as he could row when sitting down. Humor and the ability to deflect the consequence of defeat is an important element of the S-Factor that John B. clearly manifested.

After John B. returned to Philadelphia after the end of the First World War, he rededicated himself to his dream of becoming the greatest oarsman in the history of the sport despite his advancing age as an athlete. He went on to again win the U.S. championship and win 93 strait rowing races. When he bought a new scull and applied for entry to the Henley Regatta in 1920 at the age of 31, he assumed his invitation to compete would just be a formality. Due to ue to his status as the U.S. Champion. Instead he was turned down on the grounds that he was not a gentleman due to the fact that he had worked with his hands as a laborer. Rather than being crushed by this defeat, he vowed to defeat whomever won the Henley Regatta at the Olympics in Antwerp that were to be held two weeks after the Henley Regatta.

In many ways the Antwerp Olympics of 1920 had an authenticity and purity to it that is unmatched today in athletic competition.

As the day of the rowing competition dawned in Antwerp, John B. was confronted with a new obstacle to attaining his dream of becoming the best of the best in his sport. Apparently the competition was being rigged by an English member of the Olympic Committee so that John B. Kelly would be unable to compete for gold medals in both the single sculls and the doubles. John B. had entered the doubles, a two man rowing team in one scull, with his cousin Paul Costello, but the time of the doubles competition had been changed so it would be held one half hour after the singles competition. Since it was too late to lodge a protest, john B. told his cousin that he would withdrawal from the singles competition as they would have no chance to win a medal if he had to exert himself heavily in the singles. He did not want his cousin to lose his chance at a medal. His cousin Paul, however would have none of it and told him that the Irish people are with him and it would mean so much to them if he could defeat Paul Beresford, the English champion who had just won the Henley Regatta and the man who was widely considered to be the greatest oarsman in the history of the sport. John B. was very moved by his cousin's willingness to sacrifice his own chance at a medal that he vowed to beat Beresford for the Irish people and still push himself to do his best to win the doubles with his cousin.

As the race between Beresford and Kelly commenced on the historic River Scheldt an invisible string appeared to link the two sculls as neither could pull ahead of the other. The dead heat between the sculls continued until the finish line became nearer and nearer. Suddenly Kelly began to inch ahead of Beresford as his arms became pistons driving him forward as the supreme strength of his intense internal motivation and self-regulation willed him to defeat Beresford in what is now considered to be greatest contest in the history of the sport. Kelly was limp with fatigue as he was lifted from the scull by his cousin and carried to the next event on a stretcher. As the starring gun was about to go off to begin the doubles competition, Kelly was leaning limply forward, holding his oars in a weak grip. As the starting gun sounded, Kelly's grip tightened and he again became a machine propelled more by his spirit than his drained and weakened body. When the finish line was crossed and they had won , Kelly collapsed from fatigue. Later, the two cousins were greeted with a ticker tape parade on Market Street in Philadelphia as Kelly was acclaimed as the only man ever to win gold medals in an Olympics rowing competition

John B. won another gold medal at the Paris Olympics and was broadly acknowledged to be one of the great athletic heroes of the 1920's in what is now known as the golden age of American Sports. A famous picture was taken of him with Babe Ruth, Red Grange and Man of War as legends of sport. As a product of his fame he was offered the chance to be a movie star by becoming the first Tarzan, but he turned it down to start aconstruction business with ten thousand dollars he borrowed from his brothers George and Walter. The construction business was called " Kelly for Brickwork" and it became one of the largest companies of its kind in America as he amassed a great fortune. Looking for another avenue for achieving success, he turned to politics where he ran for Mayor of Philadelphia in the mid 1930's, but narrowly lost while running on a Democratic ticket in Philadelphia where Republican voters outnumbered Democratic voters by a ratio of ten to one. He appeared to have a very bright political future as he was a favorite of President Franklin Roosevelt who asked him to give his nomination speech at the Democratic national convention in Philadelphia in 1940. Despite the talk that he might some day become the first Catholic President of the United States, Kelly soon after dropped out of politics and devoted the rest of his life to helping his children find their paths to success. Clearly John B. Kelly had manifested the S-Factor sub-elements of self valuing, internal motivation and self-regulation, affective effectiveness and self-potency and success drive at the very highest levels. His self-valuing permitted to him to feel worthy of success and persist despite obstacles, failures and injustices His internal – motivation and self regulation were clearly manifested when he kept training and putting in long hours and days to be ready to succeed when the opportunity for success was present. He used his affective effectiveness to martial the push to succeed when his body appeared to be unable to do more. The loyalty he inspired in others served him well in building his business and succeeding in politics. He clearly demonstrated a high level of self-potency when he started his own business and achieved great success. His success drive was obvious in every aspect of his life as it defined him and energized his efforts to accomplish great things.

Kell (John B. Kelly, jr.)

The next Kelly I would like to focus on in this family case analysis is Kell (John B. Kelly, jr.). From the time he was born on May 24, 1927, his own success drive was in reality an extension of his father's. From the time his father built a miniature life guard stand and life guard boat for him on the beach in front of their summer home in Ocean City, New Jersey, when he was six years of age, it was clear that Kell had the mission clearly defined by his father of winning the single sculls competition at the Henley regatta to avenge the injustice of not permitting his father to compete in that venue.

Kell worshiped his father and clearly bought into the mission of winning at Henley Despite the fact that John B. Kellly was very wealthy, he insisted that his children have summer jobs to introduce them to the world of work and to help prepare them for life. Kell worked as a life guard each summer in Ocean City during his high school years and his sister Grace, the future princess, worked as a waitress at the Chatterbox Restaurant in Ocean City during her teen years.

By the time Kell was nineteen he entered the rowing competition at Henley in the single sculls event. He wanted so much to win that race to please his father, but he lost. He was in tears at the end of the race and was so upset that he had to be pulled from his scull. During the next year he began to strength his S-Factor by becoming more internally motivated and self-regulated. He now wanted to win not just for his father, but to prove something to himself. In 1947 he went back to Henley with renewed resolve and won the Diamond Scull event and went on to win the Sullivan Award as the Outstanding Amateur Athlete in America. His rowing career continued until his father died in 1960. During that time he won at Henley twice and also won an Olympic Bronze medal in 1956. After his career in sports ended as an athlete he became involved in athletics administration. As the head of the AAU (the Amateur Athletics Union) and later the President of the U.S. Olympic Committee, he helped change the structure of athletic competition in the Olympics by changing the policy of strict amateurism to allow athletes to be openly financially supported. Kell clearly saw that the prior requirement of pure amateurism as a basis for Olympics competition gave an unfair advantage to those with personal or family wealth over those who could not afford to train without income or be put in a situation where they had to take money outside the rules to support their training. For his efforts as both an athlete and athletics administrator, Kell was subsequently admitted to the Olympics Hall of Fame with his father, the only father and son tandem in that Hall of Fame. To me Kell's leadership in ending hypocrisy in amateur athletics in the U.S. and in the world was clear evidence of his self potency as a change agent.

Grace Kelly

Most of those of you who are reading this probably had no or little knowledge of who George Kelly, Walter Kelly, John B. Kelly or Kell were prior to reading this as they danced on the stage of life a long time ago. Grace danced on the stage of life a long time ago as well, but she is still remembered like Elvis or Marilyn Monroe are remembered as cultural icons who had something original about them that causes us to still be fascinated by them. Prince Wiliam's bride Kate modeled her wedding dress after the one Grace wore in the first Wedding of the Century. On the cover of the Millenium Issue of People Magazine Grace's picture was in the forefront and by far the largest among the pictures of the most celebrated women of the 20th Century. What was is it that has made the icon of Grace so compelling? What was so special about her? When she was growing up in Philadelphia and spending her summers at the family's home in Ocean City, she was hardly noticed. She was a middle child in a family where the attention was focused on her beautiful older sister Peggy or the athletic and handsome Kell. Grace in her early years was a bit overweight, quiet, shy and wore clumsy glasses. She really was not an ugly duckling, but she was not a swan either. A friend of mine who was a mascot for the lifeguards on the beach in front of the Kelly's home, told me that the lifeguards hardly looked at Grace, but they were very interested in her older sister Peggy.

By the time she reached her late teens, Grace lost weight and blossomed into a very beautiful young woman who in many ways was a product of her own intent to lose weight and refine her appearance. She knew the look she wanted and through the study of make up techniques she found a way of achieving it. It took a great deal of internal motivation and self-regulation for Grace to achieve the persona and appearance we now associate with our remembrance of her. She also had a way about her that suggested a very high level of affective effectiveness. She could read the emotional needs of others very well and make them feel comfortable and valued. She also understood her own emotions very well and used them to regulate or motivate herself. To me one of the foundations of her success drive was the hurt she felt for not being invited into Main Line Philadelphia society. Although she was beautiful and was from a very wealthy, famous family, she was not considered to be a blue blood with origins in established Philadelphia society. As a result, she was never invited to the coming out parties or the society dances. I think this motivated her to prove that she was as good and worthy of appreciation and social acceptance as any of the society girls of the Main Line. Perhaps this was one of the reasons she decided to marry a prince to make her blue blood rivals Kelly Green with envy.

Grace clearly demonstrated a high level of self -potency as she knew what she wanted and went after it. When she told her father when she was eighteen that she wanted to attend the American School of Dramatic Arts in New York in order to prepare herself to become an actress, her father opposed this because his sister, her namesake, had died while trying to succeed as an actress. John B. did not think Grace was tough enough and committed enough to endure the rejections and hardships involved in becoming a professional actress. When she persisted in wanting to go to drama school , he let her try but gave her so little money to support herself that he felt sure she would come home to her comfortable life in Philadelphia in a very short time. Instead, Grace embraced the challenge of becoming an actress and supported herself through modeling and acting in commercials while in drama school. Her internal motivation and self-regulation helped her to overcome her challenges to becoming an effective actress. She entirely changed her nasal Philadelphia accent and worked hard to develop the speech pattern we now associate with Grace. When Grace was cast in the film **High** Noon, the reviews torched her for being wooden. Due to her strong S-Factor , she did not respond to this criticism in a negative way, but used it to help her to better focus on what she needed to do to become alive and real in front of the camera.

Grace also developed a very high level of interpersonal effectiveness.. There was something very real, very nice about her in her interactions with others even when she had become a mjor film star. For example, when she was on the set of the film **To Catch a** Thief, she did not hide in her dressing room and expect star treatment. To the contrary, she often sat with the crew and sewed costumes while wearing an old sweater and no make up when scenes were being shot that did not include her. If anyone saw her they would assume she was a wardrobe mistress on the film. However, when it was nearing time for her to appear in a scene, she would go into her dressing room and transform herself in a very short time into the beautiful, stylish woman she was being asked to play.

She definitely developed a high level of self-valuing, but not in a cocky, egocentric or conceited way, but more as an inner confidence based upon the hard work that she had put into making herself worthy of success. She made everyone feel at ease, because she was at ease with herself. Just as Cary Grant had transformed Archilbald Leach into Cary Grant, Grace had transformed her once awkward self into the self we can see on the screen.

Not only did Grace use her own, very strong S-Factor as an engine for her own pursuit of success, but she further passed on the Kelly culture of success to her own children. Prince Albert, the current monarch of Monaco, has exhibited a strong S-Factor since assuming the throne and his sister Princess Caroline, has been an enduring international presence in support of Monaco for decades. It would certainly have been hard for Mary Kelly to believe that the culture of success that she built for her family in a poor row house in Philadelphia would lead to her great grand daughters being born as princesses and one of her great, great grand daughters actually being closely related to Queen Elizabeth of England. How is that for an Irish fairy tale, but that's the fascinating thing about life, one never knows how far hard work, luck or destiny will take a family if those such as Mary and John Henry are able to create a culture of success for their children.

CHAPTER 14

LEE KUAN YEW: THE FATHER OF SINGAPORE'S CULTURE OF SUCCESS

by John Taccarino

It is truly amazing what Lee Kuan Yew was able to accomplish for Singapore in creating a culture of success for an island nation that has been seldom or ever rivaled in its transformative progress in moving from a backwater colony after the Second World War to its present status as one of the true economic powerhouses in the world today. I have adapted this chapter from a chapter on Lee Kwan Yew that appeared in my earlier book "S-(Success) Factor, the Psychological Roots of Success." (Taccarino et al, 2015.). Although Lee Kuan Yew has now passed away after a long , productive life , his spirit and legacy of S-Factor strength will endure as will the culture of success that he created in Singapore. In many ways a chapter on Lee Kuan Yew is a perfect segue to the next section of this book that deals with the importance of morality and ethics as key and essential accompaniment to S-Factor strength in building bases for enduring success.

L ee Kuan Yew had for over fifty years been one of the most effective political and moral leaders in recent world history. He is generally viewed as the father of modern Singapore. From the time he was born in Singapore in 1923 until his death 2014, he has seen Singapore transform from a backwater British colony primarily supported by rubber plantations and low income immigrant workers into one of the most successful economies and nations in the world. Much of that transformation has been advanced by the work and policies of Lee Kuan Yew in the 25 years he served as Singapore's Prime Minister after breaking from British rule. The People's Action Party, the political party Lee Kuan Yew helped form, has held elected power in Singapore since its formation as an independent country. Although there have been criticisms of its authoritarian policies, Lee Kuan Yew had clearly helped to found a culture of success in Singapore. It definitely is a country that works which is certainly not the case in many countries in the world today. As Lee Kuan Yew had suggested, Singapore's greatest resource is the work ethic of its people. His policies and the policies of his successors have created an environment of racial fairness and moral leadership in a very diverse country that has a Chinese majority and large representations of individuals of Indian, Caucasian, Malaysian and Eurasian heritages. It has become one of the leading business centers in the world with the third highest per capita income. It rates at or near the top among all world countries in health care, safety, good government and economic opportunity.

In many ways Lee Kuan Yew used the strength of his own S-Factor and the moral foundations of his teachings to create a culture of S-Factor Strength in Singapore. I would now like to analyze Lee Kuan Yew's own S-Factor in a way that may help to explain how he was able to use the strength and tendencies of his own S-Factor to create a culture of shared S-Factor and moral strength in Singapore.

Self -Valuing

Lee Kuan Yew earned his sense of self -value through hard work and accomplishment. His grandfather was the managing director of a steam ship company based in Singapore in the early part of the twentieth century, but much of his wealth was lost in the Great Depression, There was , however, enough money still available to allow Lee Kuan Yew to study at Cambridge University in England where he achieved great academic success and later studied law at the Fizwilliam College of Cambridge. The confidence he gained by excelling at Cambridge served him well when he returned to Singapore and led the struggle for independence from Great Britain. He was not only confident in his own abilities, but also confident in the ability of Singapore to stand alone and succeed without British assistance. His policies as the first Prime Minister of Singapore clearly sought to imbue a sense of pride, moral integrity and a sense of personal effectiveness in the people of Singapore.

Internal Motivation and Self-regulation

Things were not easy in Singapore when Lee Kuan Yew survived the Japanese occupation during World War II or in the years of struggle that brought Singapore's break from Great Britain and its eventual achievement of sovereignty. Lee Kuan Yew had to be motivated from within the by the foundation of his moral strength to persist and be resilient in the face of setbacks and obstacles as the path to self rule for Singapore was not an easy one to travel. He needed to be self-regulated to maintain his focus and keep his dream alive for the future of the Singapore people. When he did come to power as the Prime Minster of Singapore, he saw the importance of putting in place policies that supported internal- motivation and self-regulation within his people. He also had to make the case for the moral right of the people of Singapore to achieve self rule. When self rule was achieved he then sought to create a culture of success for its people. At that point he challenged and encouraged the people of Singapore to start businesses and discipline themselves to support their commerce. Lee Kuan Yew clearly saw the role of government as helping to put its people in a position to succeed if they were self-motivated, self disciplined and willing to work hard no matter if they were Chinese, Indian, Malasian, or Eurasian or Caucasian in origin.

Affective Effectiveness

Although Lee Kuan Yew could certainly be very analytical and logical in this thought processes and planning, he also had a high level of affective effectiveness. He was both able to read the emotions of others and use his own affect to be a source of internal motivation when needed. As an effective politician, he was able to tap into the emotional needs and unexpressed feelings of his people in ways that gave them a voice.. Part of being an effective political leader is to understand not just what is said, but what is felt by those he is representing and to be responsive to the feelings and emotional needs of even his opponents who needed to be understood as well. In helping to build a culture of success in Singapore. Pursuantly, Lee Kuan

Yew sought to channel the emotional needs and wants of his people in ways that fostered productivity and accomplishment on a sustainable and long term basis..

Interpersonal Effectiveness

Lee Kuan Yew had a truly an amazing level of interpersonal effectiveness. It certainly required an extremely high level of interpersonal effectiveness to build the coalitions with those ofdiffering political philosophies in the years that led up Singapore's independence from Great Britain. It took a great deal interpersonal effectiveness to engage in diplomatic interactions with world leaders and build the constituencies that kept his party in power for so many years in Singapore. It certainly required a high level of interpersonal effectiveness to build the personal relationships and friendships that are essential for any government to work on a small island. Additionally, the ability to develop and foster relationships in politics allowed Lee Kuan Yew to seamlessly pass on the baton of power in Singapore to his successors. It was also the valuing of interpersonal effectiveness that helped Lee Kuan Yew to create the sense of working together and puling together as a people that is so important for a country with few natural resources to find resources for success in an international economy. In many ways it was the support for interpersonal effectiveness in Singapore that Lee Kuan Yew helped to create that has made Singapore a favorite place for business for many people in the world today.

On the international stage, Lee Kuan Yew used his dominant S-Factor to provide moral leadership and counsel all nations of Southeast Asia to seek cooperative relationships where all parties can succeed. In the book, *lee Kwan Yew, The Grand Mater's Insights on China, the United States and the World.* Lee Kwan Yew presented a very interesting perspective on Sino-U.S, relations. "Unlike U.S.-Soviet relations during the Cold War, there is no irreconcilable ideological conflict between the United States and a China that has enthusiastically embraced the market. Sino-American relations are both cooperative and competitive. Competition between them is inevitable, but conflict is not. After the collapse of the Soviet Union, the United States and China are more likely to view each other as competitors if not adversaries. But the die has not been cast. The best possible outcome is a new understanding that when they cannot cooperate, they will coexist and allow all countries in the Pacific to grow and thrive." In light of the increased tension between the United States and China in the area of the South China sea, the words of Lee Kuan Yew appear particularly important now from both from both a moral and political perspective as a war between the United States and China would be a tragedy of shared consequences for all involved as all parties have so much more to gain from the search for peace and mutual benefit as Lee Kuan Yew would tell us.

Self Potency

Throughout his career Lee Kuan Yew has taken the initiative to change things and try to make a better world for himself and the people of Singapore by initiating incremental bases for economic and cultural advancement and improvement.. As in all political decisions and governments, there may not always have been agreement on his policies, but he never shied away from challenges and the pull of the status quo. Sometimes self potency is manifested in not just doing something, but avoiding something. It often involves being able to look over the horizon of life events and see something coming, that others do not see. This could involve acting upon an opportunity or it could also involve taking action to avoid something that is potentially very harmful or dangerous. During the Japanese occupation of Singapore in World War II Lee Kuan Yew was on a list of men to be segregated and moved to another place on the island, but he convinced the guard who had come to take him away to let him go home to change his clothes before leaving for the destination. By not returning until it the group of men had been taken away, he avoided what would have become his death sentence. The next day he learned that all the men who been taken away that day had been executed. Self -potency is often about not just acting, but taking the right actions at the right time. In the transformation of Singapore Lee Kuan Yew in many cases made the right decisions and took the right actions at the right time. This obviously is a key element of leadership and effective self -potency.

Beyond his own self- potency, Lee Kuan Lee has clearly instilled self- potency as a key element of the culture of Singapore. The people of Singapore are clearly among those in the world who try to make things happen and are not afraid to take creative chances and assume risks to make things better and build a dynamic culture for meaningful and effective living.

Success Drive

Throughout his life Lee Kuan Yew had manifested a clear drive to succeed, not just for himself, but for those he was seeking to assist. Success is never easy as it takes hard work and perseverance. A strong success drive also kept someone such as Lee Kuan Lee on target and on mission. For Lee Kuan Yew the primary mission in his life had been to advance the moral fibre and success of Singapore by instilling both the need to achieve and the effort to achieve. The success drive Lee Kuan Yew helped to instill in the culture of Singapore helped to transform a small island in an economic backwater into what it is today. Thanks to the culturally based success drive that Lee Kuan Yew helped to instill, Singapore shares the cultures of success found in other great economic centers of the world such as Hong Kong, New York, Shanghai, London and Chicago.

PART 4

Morality, Ethics and the S-Factor

In education it is essential to not only develop S-Factor strength in students, but also to ground that development upon a strong foundation of ethical and moral values. A strong S-Factor can be a powerful tool that can be used in the service of either good or evil. It is important for students to understand the importance of moral and ethical values in the context of the uses of a strong S-Factor. The following case studies are examples of tools for helping student to analyze and grasp the differences in how S-Factor strength can be used in the service of humanity by someone such as Winston Churchil and how S-Factor strength can be used for the destruction of humanity if one's ethical and moral values become corrupted as was the case of Adolf Hitler. It also seeks to identify the importance of balancing the development of S-Factor strength with the need to develop a moral compass in pursuing success in any area of life.

CHAPTER 15

HITLER'S S-FACTOR STRENGTH AND MORAL DECAY

By John Taccarino and John Leonard

This chapter was adapted from a chapter in the book "The Choices of the Soul" (Taccarino et al, 2017) titled "The Contrasting Choices of Tilly Frankl and Adolf Hitler." It provides an important lesson to students regarding how the development of S-Factor strength can be corrupted by moral decay as was the case with Adolf Hitler.

How did Adolf Hitler, the academic underachiever, secondary school drop out and failed artist, become the Fuhrer of Germany? How did the man who is generally seen as one of the most evil men in the history of our world achieve such infamy? When he was homeless and sleeping on park benches or living in Jewish run social service hostels in Vienna prior to World War !, would his Jewish friends have believed that he could and would become *Time Magazine 's* "Man of the Year" in 1938. Would the upper class Jewish family in Vienna who entertained a quiet, socially awkward, poorly dressed Hitler in their home for an evening of music have welcomed him so pleasantly if they knew he would later become the agent of their destruction (Hamann, 1999) . Would the Jewish art dealer who befriended Hitler when no one else would buy his paintings have believed that Hitler could become incarnate evil, the dark devil of death for himself and the Jewish people. In reality the Hitler of Vienna was not the transformed Hitler of Munich and Berlin who manifested a dominant S-Factor. Unfortunately the new Hitler lost his moral compass in the process of transforming and strengthening his S-Factor.

In Vienna Hitler had a very weak S-Factor, but he was not evil or necessarily inclined toward evil acts. He had a very weak sense of self –valuing perhaps due to his father's verbal and physical abuse wjen younger.. As a child he turned his anger toward his father inward and repressed his rage. He came to feel inferior, worthless and humjliated by his inability to effectively respond or to protect himself from his father's abuse. When he saw his mother beaten by his father, this only further reinforced his sense of impotence and humiliation when he could not protect her either. (Miller, 1980)

His sense of inferiority and humiliation appeared to block the development of the S-Factor elements of internal motivation and self- regulation to the extent that he did poorly in school despite being bright. He seemed to be drifting and was unable to demonstrate resilience in response to his failures as a student and as an artist.

His repressed anger and humiliation from the beatings he received his father blunted the development of the S-Factor element of affective effectiveness. He also tended to overreact to criticism and often displayed fits of anger when he was criticized or became frustrated by a lack of success.

With regard to the S-Factor element of interpersonal effectiveness, Hitler had few friends and lacked the ability to effectively interact with others or be persuasive in group settings. His feelings of inferiority and a fear of failure also inhibited the development of self potency as he seldom took initiative or acted upon an opportunity in a positive and assertive manner. Although he had a strong need and desire to succeed, he feared failure to the point that his success drive remained dormant as a catalyst for performance.

When World War I broke out in 1914 he did not wish to serve in the Austro-Hungarian army so he decided to go to Munich to enlist in the German army. For the first time in his life he found a place where he felt that he belonged. He liked and found purpose in the army. His performance assessments judged him to be a good soldier who exhibited courage. He was awarded the Iron Cross, a medal for valor, but he was judged by his superiors to be lacking in leadership qualities and he never rose above the rank of corporal in his four years in the army. His life changed, however, when he was exposed to mustard gas in a battle in Belgium and was transported to a military hospital. Hitler was diagnosed as exhibiting "war fatigue" and "hysterical blindness" (hysterical blindness does not have a physical causation, but has a psychological etiology). (Kershaw, 1999, pp. 97 and 102)" War fatigue" refers to a mental state later called brief reactive psychosis. A person experiencing brief reactive psychosis may experience psychotic like hallucinations, but the condition is considered temporary and associated with exposure to a traumatic event. Being exposed to mustard gas and nearly dying would appear to be traumatic enough to qualify as a cause of Hitler's psychologically rooted blindness. During Hitler's stay at Passewalk Military Hospital, his sight returned, but he instantly became blind again when he learned that Germany had surrendered. He was assessed and treated by a Dr. Forster who, based upon the treatments practices at the time, likely used hypnosis and shock treatment. It is difficult to determine the specifics of Hitler's diagnosis and the treatment received, as Dr. Foster committed suicide after being interrogated by members of the Gestapo after Hitler came to power and all records pertaining Hitler's stay at the hospital in Passewalk were destroyed. Hitler later wrote in his book "Mein Kampf " (1943)that he had experienced a spiritual awakening while in the hospital in which it was revealed to him by God that he was to become the savior of Germany as its leader. (Kershaw, 1999, pp. 97 and 102) Whether it was a spiritual revelation from a dark angel impersonating God, , a hallucination, hypnotic suggestion or the consequence of shock therapy, Hitler was inspired and immediately set upon the task of seeking to transform himself into a person worthy of leading Germany. Hitler began trying to become a more effective person by seeking to transform his personality weaknesses into strengths. Within a year's time the Hitler who had always been awkward and quiet in social situation, had suddenly become a powerful orator that could rouse the emotions and loyal fervor of the thousands who cheered his speeches in political rallies. As Hitler moved forward in his political career the personality elements of his S-Factor became stronger and stronger.

To assess the strength of Hitler's transformed S-Factor, we can use a series of questions that are employed in the book

S(Success) Factor : thePsycholgical Roots of Success to (Taccarino, et al 2015, pages 18-22) to assess his overall level of S-Factor strength and his strength as it relates to the various elements of the S-Factor. The number of "no" responses to the following questions will be used to identify Hitler's position on the S-Factor continuum. Since you are not here with me I will provide my assessments, but you can keep score as well. You may not agree with me, but let's try it out.

INVENTORYING THE RELATIVE STRENGTH OF YOUR S-FACTOR ELEMENTS

I will try to respond to the questions as Hitler likely would have responded after he had gone through his S-Factor transformation in the years following World War I..

Self-Valuing

Do you feel worthy of love, respect and success? *Yes*

Do you value your life, accomplishments and goals? *Yes, if he responded to the assessment in 1938*

Do you truly value and respect who you are? *Yes, he saw himself as the savior of Germany.*

Do you see your ideal self as close to the actual self you know yourself to be? *Yes, he believed in his superiority*

Are you resilient in dealing with failure and persistent in seeking to accomplish what you feel truly worthy of accomplishing? *Yes, he bounced back from failure of the Beer Hall*

Putsch to renew and succeed in his efforts to become the leader of Germany.

If you have the talent to achieve a goal that that it important to you, do you really believe you will achieve it? *Yes, he firmly believed he was on a mission of historic importance*

If you answered yes to all of these questions, you are clearly manifesting S-Factor strength in this area.

If you answered no to at least three of these questions, this is an area where you are clearly manifesting S-Factor weakness.

INTERNAL MOTIVATION AND SELF-REGULATION

Are you motivated from within? *Yes*

Are you a self –starter? *Yes*

Can you persist at tasks when you are not being praised or getting immediate rewards for your efforts? *Yes*

Do you have an internal locus of control that is expressed in self- discipline and the ability to keep your cool under pressure? *Yes*

Do you clearly avoid procrastination? *Yes*

Are you resilient in the face of failure and persistent in completing tasks even when things are not going well? *Yes, or at least until things started going badly with the collapse of the Russian front*

Are you generally able to control your emotions, particularly anger? *No, Hitler appeared to control his emotions in public, but his rant in his bunker in Berlin when the Russians were knocking on his door was legendary.*

Are you able to avoid or stop doing things that you know are bad for you? *No, he must have known the possible consequences of his evil acts, but he still carried them out*

If you answered yes to all of these questions, you are clearly manifesting S-Factor strength in this area.

If you answered no to at least four of these questions, this is an area where you are clearly manifesting S-Factor weakness.

AFFECTIVE EFFECTIVENESS

Are you able to regulate your emotions in your work and in your interactions with others? *Yes*

Are you able to focus and use your emotions to motivate yourself to succeed when others are trying to discourage you or when you are experiencing failure? *Yes*

Are you able to think outside the box and find creative solutions to difficult problems? *Yes, his plan for invading France was certainly outside the box*

Are you able to read and respond effectively to the emotional needs and responses of others? *Yes, that was his strength in being able to play upon the dark biases and revenge needs of the crowds he addressed*

Do you have compassion for the feelings and needs of most of the people that you know? *No*

Are you able to avoid angry outbursts even when you have been wronged? *No*

.

If you answered yes to all of these questions, you are clearly manifesting S-Factor strength in this area.

If you answered no to at least three of these questions, this is an area where you are clearly manifesting S-Factor weakness.

INTERPERSONAL EFFECTIVENESS

Are you persuasive and able to effectively communicate your ideas and needs to others? *Yes, just ask the crowds at Nuremburg*

Do you enjoy social interactions with others? *Yes*

Are you self-assured and poised in social interactions? *Yes*

Do people tend to see you as a leader? *Yes, finding a way to become the leader of Germany kind of answers that one*

Do you smile and make eye contact with people in social or work situations? *Yes, his hypnotic stare was legendary*

Do you make people feel special and important when you are talking with them? *Yes*

Do the people you know well sometimes seek your advice in personal matters? Yes

Do you tend to be a good listener? *No*

If you answered yes to all of these questions, you are clearly manifesting S-Factor strength in this area.

If you answered no to at least three of these questions, this is an area where you are clearly manifesting S-Factor weakness.

SELF POTENCY

Are you a self-starter who makes things happen? *Yes, he was great at starting wars*

Do you have the courage to try when there are clear consequences for failure? *Yes*

Are you a glass half full type of person in dealing with life problems? *Yes*

Do you have the potential to be an effective leader? *Yes, he was a powerful leader, but unfortunately he led his country in a horrifically wrong direction*

Do you tend to persist when other people quit when performing a task? *Yes*

Are you more of an actor than a reactor when faced with an obstacle or difficult problem? *Yes*

If you answered yes to all of these questions, you are clearly manifesting S-Factor strength in this area.

If you answered no to at least three of these questions, this is an area where you are clearly manifesting S-Factor weakness.

SUCCESS DRIVE

Do you have a strong work ethic? *Yes*

Do you persist, or even work harder, when failures mount? *Yes*

Do you have a passion to succeed in a personal, academic or work area that is important to you? *Yes*

Are you willing to pay the price of success and make sacrifices to succeed? *Yes*

Do you truly believe you will succeed in an area of life that is the most important to you? *Yes*

Do you believe you are only a failure when you do not try? Yes

If you answered yes to all of these questions, you are clearly manifesting S-Factor strength in this area.

If you answered no to at least three of these questions, this is an area where you are clearly manifesting S-Factor weakness.

S-FACTOR ASSESSMENT OUTCOME FOR HITLER

By my counting I have 4 "no" responses. This would place Hitler in the highest range in terms of his overall S-Factor strength. How did you see it?

After Hitler had gone through his S-Factor transformation he achieved self-valuing, but unfortunately it soon morphed into an exaggerated belief in his superiority. In his book Mein Kampf it was clear that Hitler was clearly seeking to erect a more confident, more successful Hitler. He began to demonstrate the emergence of internal motivation and self-regulation. After World War I ended he remained in the army and took an assignment as an army intelligence agent seeking to infiltrate the German Workers Party. Hitler soon stopped being a spy and began working actively for the party. At this time he began giving speeches to gain recruits for the party. Suddenly Hitler found there was something he was really good at. He found that he could connect with crowds and move them by the power of his increasingly persuasive oratory. His self confidence began to soar as crowds became larger and more enthusiastic in listening to and reacting to what he was saying. After he joined the NAZI party and became its leader, the crowds became larger still. He soon began to achieve a sense of what themes moved the masses. He was becoming a politician and was developing his affective effectiveness to the point that he was becoming more and adept at reading the emotions of his audiences and learning what could trigger the emotional response and fervor he was seeking. He was also able to channel his own emotions as a rage against the Jews and Communists as betrayers of Germany. He soon was able to create a hypnotic effect within his audience through his fervent rants against the Jews, The Treaty of Versailles and the Communists,. In a relatively short period of time he achieved a tremendously powerful connection that resonated with the conscious and unconscious thoughts, emotions and needs of his growing number of followers. The famed Psychiatrist Karl Jung observed that Hitler was "first man to tell every German what he has been thinking and feeling all along in his unconscious about German fate, especially since the defeat in the World War". (Knikerbocker (1941)

Alfons Heck, a former member of the Hitler Youth commented on what it was like when he first heard Hitler at a rally . "We erupted into a frenzy of nationalistic pride that bordered on hysteria. For minutes on end, we shouted at the top of our lungs, with tears streaming down our faces: *Sieg Heil, Sieg Heil, Sieg Heil!* From that moment on, I belonged to Adolf Hitler body and soul. (Heck (1985).

It was clear at this point that Hitler had learned how to play his audiences like a musical instrument. He was well on his way to becoming an important leader of Germany, , but he had to decide what type of leader he wanted to become and where he was seeking to take the NAZI party. Was he going to take the high rode of appealing to the best of the German people by inspiring them to seek greatness in the justice of their causes and to inspire them to work for the good of all nations and a shared humanity. He could have used the power of his oratory and the emerging strength of his S-Factor in providing a type of ethical, moral constructive leadership that may have gained for him an exalted place in the history of Germany and the world. Instead, he chose to take the very lowest road of moral and ethical corruption by seeking to use racial hatred and the rage of a humiliated people as the platform of evil for his political ambitions. What any political leader needs to understand is that one's choices will generally determine outcomes. Just before Hitler became Chancellor of Germany in 1933 he still had a choice. His anit-semitism was still mostly rhetoric. His party had run on a platform of economic renewal, the repudiation of the Treaty of Versailles, jobs creation and anti-communism. The consequences of the Great Depression and the fear of a communist take over were much bigger issues to the German people than the achievement of Aryan supremacy or a desire to rid the country of the Jews. In reality the economic revival of the country could have been greatly aided by German Jews who were skilled businessmen, bankers and entrepreneurs. What was so bizarre about Hitler's thinking in 1933 was that in seeking to build a culture of success in Germany he was also seeking to exclude a small segment of that population who could have contributed so much to his dream of building a stronger Germany through hard work, self-discipline, and the shared desire to excel. If he was also seeking to build military power, he certainly needed the services of the world's best scientists. The irony is that the world's best nuclear physicists and the very scientists who would become primarily responsible for developing the atomic bomb and the H bomb were all professors at the University of Gottingen in Germany in 1933. Unfortunately from Hitler's perspective, Dr. Leo Szilard, the man who had already conceived the concept of the nuclear chain reaction was Jewish as was Albert Teller, the man who would become the father of the H bomb. The other great physicist who was on the faculty of the University of Gottenburg at that time was Enrico Fermi, an Italian who had a Jewish wife whom he loved and wished to protect. Hitler then made one of the great mistakes in history by allowing his expressed hatred of Jews to outweigh what should have been the correct military decision of doing anything he could to employ these scientists in the service of the nation's armaments program. Against all reason, Hitler launched a purge against these scientists at the University of Gottengen who were associated with Einstein's "Jewish physics." As a result of Hitler's actions and the anti-Jewish laws that soon came into place, all three of these men fled Germany. Why Hitler allowed them to leave knowing they could be of great value to its enemies is very difficult to understand from the perspective of Nazi evil and its capacity for ruthlessness. So instead of the " jewish Physics " of Einstein, Teller, Fermi and Szilard that could have produced operational nuclear weapons for Germany's military, there was a commitment to the "Aryan or German Physics" of Johannes Strack, who I believe won Nobel Prize in Stupidity. In " German Physics" was the speed of lighter faster or did gravity cause limburger cheese to melt. Did the Earth gravitate around Himmler's head? If Hitler had still been living and had visited Hiroshima in 1945, I am sure he would have gotten a big bang out of a product of "jewish Physics." In any case, scientific progress in the area of nuclear physics essentially ground to a halt until the late 1930's when German scientists were finally given permission to to use " Jewish physics" in there work. Soon after being allowed to use " Jewish Physics" Otto Hahn and Fritz Strassman achieved nuclear fission in their laboratory. This advancement triggered the start of Germany's nuclear bomb program. Fortunately the program was only in existence for a couple of months as many of the scientists involved in the program were enlisted in the German army during the invasion of Poland and the resources needed to push the program forward were diverted for other purposes such as building more concentration camps. The scary thing is that German scientists were very close to being able to produce a chain reaction which would be precursor necessary for building a nuclear reactor and assembling an operational atomic bomb. The scientist were correct in identifying uranium and carbon as the key elements for producing a nuclear chain reaction (the key next step before being able to assemble an atom bomb), but they failed to produce a chain because they were using a poor grade of carbon.

Tormented by the plight of Jews in Jews Germany , Dr. Szilard, a man with a an extremely strong S-Factor, used his self-potency to take the initiative in 1939 to write a letter to President Roosevelt that Professor Einstein, another German Jew, signed. The letter warned President Roosevelt that the Nazi 's were seeking to develop a nuclear bomb and that such a bomb could be built and that they had identified the correct materials to build it. The letter warned that the United States needed to counter the German threat by immediately launching a secret program to build an atomic bomb of its own. Unfortunately Roosevelt procrastinated in committing to the nuclear bomb project until after Germany declared war against he United States. Soon after the Manhattan Project was finally launched in 1942, Dr, Szilard and Enrico Fermi, his former colleague at The University of Gottingen, created the first nuclear chain reaction by using the same materials, carbon and uranium that the German scientists had been using, but in their case they employed a purer form of carbon. Within three years the atomic bombs that were produced by the Manhattan Project were detonated at Hiroshima and Nagasaki. By 1949 through the work of Albert Teller, the United States had an operational hydrogen bomb. What is of concern from a historical perspective is why Franklin Roosevelt delayed the start of the Manhattan Project until 1942 despite pleas from Einstein and Szilard regarding the danger Hitler represented to Jews and humanity. If the Manhattan Project had been started in 1939 rather than 1942, how many of the lives of Jews and Allied soldiers could have been saved if the atomic bomb was available for use in 1942 to force a Nazi surrender.

The question of why Hitler's decided to drive from Germany the scientists it needed the most was perhaps best answered by Hannah Arendt in her book **The Origins of Totaliarianism** (Arendt 1966) in which she contends that Hitler was preparing for two wars when he gained power. One war was to be waged against the nations seen as enemies of Germany. The other war was a war against the Jewish people. Apparently the war against the Jewish people had a higher priority for Hitler and the Nazi Party than the national goals of Germany as Hitler clearly needed Szilard, Fermi and Teller to develop the nuclear weapons that would have given Germany its only chance for victory against what became the Allied Armies backed by populations at least six times the size of Germany's.

Instead of using his strong S-Factor productively and making choices that were inclusive of German Jews in seeking to build a nation and a culture of shared success., Hitler chose to build a police state culture of evil, failure and eventual ruination for all. Instead of creating a win/win outcome for all Germans, he created a lose/lose outcome of death and destruction for both German Jews and those Germans who were not Jewish.

The logic behind the racial theories of Hitler was so appallingly flawed that they would be considered laughable if their consequences did not prove to be so horrific. The evil war Hitler was conducting against the Jews was so vulnerable to satire that Charlie Chaplain in his 1940 film **The Great Dictator** reduced the essence of Hitler to that of a ridiculous caricature. Chaplin later said that he would never have made the picture if he had understood the full horror and evil of Hitler's efforts to exterminate Jews in Germany and in the nations his forces occupied.The only thing worse than the outcomes of Hitler's evil that were manifested, were the outcomes that could have been manifested if Hitler had chosen to prepare for a war that could lead to world domination before he began his war against the Jewish people. Let's go back to 1933 and see what level of evil could have been wrought if Hitler temporarily ceased his attacks upon Jews and sought to enlist them in the service of his preparation for a war aimed at world domination. Using the timetable for developing nuclear weapons that were achieved by the Manhattan Project through the services of Szilard, Fermi and Teller, it is possible that if Hitler began his nuclear arms development program in 1933 rather than embarking on his war against Jews, he could conceivably have had operational atomic bombs at his disposal by 1937 and operational hydrogen bombs at his disposal by 1940. Could one imagine the consequences of Hitler having the hydrogen bomb? The Battle of Britain would have been over in a day with the whole of London in smoldering ruins. The Red Army would have had no chance in the Battles of Stalingrad and Moscow if H bombs were deployed by the Nazi forces. Hitler then could have begun his delayed war against the Jews on a much larger scale. If the Luffwaffe attacked New York City , the city with the largest population of Jews in world, with a hydrogen bomb more than five times the entire population of Jews in Germany could have been killed in a single moment. The history of the world could have been greatly altered and a dark age of Nazi evil would have extended throughout the world. Thank God this did not happen. The key thing that may have saved the Jewish people and humanity in general from the full consequences of Hitler's evil, was the greed of evil itself. The greed of evil seeks immediate gratification and Hitler's greed for immediate and easily achievable dominance over the Jewish people of Germany appeared to have superseded any hint of even Machiavellian logic as a basis for his decisions.

Learning How to Succeed

Was Hitler a Madman?

Many people just assume Hitler was a madman because it would seem to require a person to be mad or insane to do the evil things that he did. Some of the most notable and psychiatrists in the world such as Freud, Fromm and Frankl have offered their opinions on the topic of Hitler's mental state or states., but there is no clear consensus of opinion. In his insightful book **Hitler; Diagnosis of a destructive** Prophet (Redlich 1988), the neurologist and psychiatrist Fritz Redlich gave the opinion that the paranoid delusions Hitler exhibited *"could be seen as symptoms of a mental disorder, but the largest part of the personality worked normal."* Hitler *"knew what he what he was doing and he did it with pride and enthusiasm."* The great psychologist Erik Erikson essentially supported this viewpoint in his book **Childhood and Society** (Erikson, 1950) when he observed that although Hitler did exhibit certain mental pathologies, he was able to control them and use them for his own purposes.

These perspectives on Hitler are entirely consistent with my own observation that the level of S-Factor strength that Hitler exhibited could have allowed him to control and deal with his underlying delusions and mental disorders. It is possible that he even channeled his paranoid delusions in ways that added fire, focus and theme to his oratory. Hitler's use of his S-Factor strengths could have assisted him as it has assisted others in dealing with addictions and underlying mental disorders and still be successful.

Perhaps it is better that Hitler is not judged to be a madman as his madness might be seen as an excuse for the great evil of his theories, actions and behavior. Perhaps it is better to just let him rot in the historical infamy of his self-created hell. Let Hitler be a cautionary tale for those who might seek to use the strengths of their S-Factors in the service of great evil and for those who might vote for such a person. Thank God for those such as Dr. Leo Szilard and Dr. Einstein who used the strength of their own very strong S-Factors to push back against the great evil of Hitler.

The Paradoxical Effect of Hitler in Furthering Racial Tolerance and Understanding

In pursuing racist evil to its extremes Hitler may have produced the paradoxical effect of making tamer racists ashamed to be racists or at least be ashamed to display their racism openly or in a way that obstructs the freedoms of other races and ethnic groups. The the gentleman's agreements in the U.S. during the 1930's were certainly tamer forms of racism than that practiced by Hitler, but they still represented racism. The shame and guilt many tamer racists may have experienced when the full horrors of the Holocaust were finally revealed, may have had significantly positive effects in changing racial attitudes and understandings in America and elsewhere for the better. When I visited the Holocaust Museum in Berlin with my son and saw what I saw, it is hard for me to conceive that anyone could still be a racist and still be a cogent human

REFERENCES

Arendt, Hannah (1966). "The Origins of Totalitrianism" New York: Harcourt Brace and World

Erikson, Erik (1950),"Childhood and Society." Cambridge, Massachusetts: Winthrop

Hamman, Brigitte (1999), "Hitler's Vienna: A Dictator's Apprenticeship." New York: Oxford University Press

Heck, Alfons (1985) " A Child of Hitler: Germany in the Days When God Wore a Swastika." Phoenix: Renaissance House

Hitler, Adolf: Ralph Mannheim.(1943) "Mein Kampf." Boston: Houghton Mifflin

Kershaw, Ian (1999). "Hitler-1889-1936: Hubris." New York: Norton

Knickerbocker, H.R. (1941). "Is Tomorrow Hitler?" New York: Reynal and Hitchcock

Miller, Alice (1980. "For Your Own Good." New York: Norton

Redlich, Fritz (1998). " Hitler: Diagnosis of a Destructive Prophet." New York: Oxford University Press

Taccarino, J. et al (2015) S(Success) Factor, the Psychological Roots of Success." Melbourne, Florida: Motival Press

Taccarino, j. et al (2017) "." The Choices of the Soul." Melbourne, Florida,: Motivational Press

CHAPTER 16

WINSTON CHURCHILL

By Rachel Bomher

This chapter was contributed by Rachel Bomher. The chapter is important as success did not come easily to Winston Churchill in the early stages of his life. but he learned how to succeed. Any student who is underachieving and not realizing his/her potential can draw inspiration from Churchill as he found ways of overcame his pattern of underachievement by developing a strong S-Factor. Winston was clearly an underachiever, but he overcame these early tendencies and learned how succeed to the point that he has now been acclaimed as the greatest person in the history of England. Although Churchil was not a morally and ethically perfect person, his extremely strong S-Factor was grounded on a strong foundation of moral and ethical principles and values that he consistently sought to manifest in his very public life and career. When he did go off course from the direction of his moral compass, he consistently tried to make amends and get back on the course defined by his moral compass. This is an S-Factor and moral trait certainly worth

encouraging in students as they seek to strengthen their S-Factors.

The history of the 20th century was greatly influenced by the political leadership of Hitler, and Churchill. The actions of these men whether for good or evil, completely changed the course of the modern world. Both of these individuals developed very strong S-Factors, but they used there S-Factors in much different ways. Churchill became a beacon of moral strength for his people in their darkest hours and ultimately lead them and their allies to victory against Hitler's forces of evil in World II.

Winston Churchill, like Hitler, did not have a strong S-Factor in his youth. He continually struggled to thrive, academically and politically.

Family, Childhood, and Education

Coming from a military dynasty, Winston Churchill's mind was filled will military ideology and tactic since he was a young boy. He was born in 1874 at his families' large palace, Blenheim, in Britain. His ancestors were both British and American. His father was the British Lord Randolph Churchill and his paternal grandfather was the 7th Duke of Marlborough. Winston's ancestor, John Churchill, made military history by winning many battles for Queen Anne 200 years earlier. His mother's ancestors were Americans who fought for the independence of the American colonies in George Washington's armies (Churchill Center, 2007). However, because his father was a politician and his mother was often preoccupied, they did not have much time for their son. A nanny, Mrs. Everest, raised Winston and he loved her dearly.

As a child, Winston was described as being willful, stubborn and adventurous, He often got into trouble.(Lyons, P. 1). In his father's opinion he "'lacked cleverness, knowledge and any capacity for settled work. He has a great talent for show-off, exaggeration and make-believe'" (Keegan, P. 2). Young Winston loved reading and playing with toy soldiers in his room. It was on one of these occasions that his father made a rare visit to his room and saw his toys. Winston told him of his desire to join the army and expressed the opinion that "becoming a solider was a good way of earning distinction." However, this could have been an attempt to impress his father, as his disapproval surely hit Winston hard (Lyons, P. 2). Winston thus made it his life's work to not only prove his father wrong about his abilities, but to succeed where his father failed in Parliament many years before.

This was not going to be an easy task for Winston to accomplish though, as he was certainly not a model student. In 1888, he attended Harrow School, a boy's school near London. Winston found his years at Harrow challenging as he was not thought of as a good student and his teachers did not think he would go very far in life (Churchill Center, 2007). However, he did have an uncanny ability to memorize lines as he won a competition for reciting a poem from memory (Churchill Center, 2007). The only upside to his academic failures at Harrow was that Winston "realized that failure was something to be overcome and not crushed by" (Heffer P. 2). His academic failures followed him further in life when he applied to the Royal Military Academy at Sandhurst, but failed the entrance exam three times before he finally was admitted (Lyons, P. 2). However, it was at Sandhurst that Winston first tasted success. Something in the culture of success provided by Sandhurst triggered a clear transformation and strengthening of his S-Factor. He began to begin valuing himself and displaying internal motivation and self- regulation in his life and academic pursuits. He was learning all of the things that interested him most, such as "tactics, fortification, topography, military law and military fortification. Churchill graduated from Sandhurst in 1894 with honors, finishing eighth in his class of 150 students. This was a complete shift in his academic career and this allowed him to further advance his goals of proving his father wrong by achieving success as a soldier and as a politician.

Military Journalism

Soon after graduating from Sandhurst, Churchill began to exhibit a high level of self potency and a strong success drive. He was very eager to begin his military career, but no opportunities were readily available . Seeking another path to successs, he used his family's name to his advantage and traveled as an observer to Cuba, where a guerilla war was taking place between rebels and their Spanish rulers. With not much to do and desperately wanting to be on the front lines, Churchill joined the London Daily Graphic to provide reports from the front (Lyons, P. 3). His knack for writing paid off and he earned his first medal from the military, the Spanish Cross of the Order of Military Merit, and a much needed income (Lyons, P. 3). He continued to write for the rest of his life, writing a total of over 43 books (Churchill Center, 2007).

Winston's first official military posting was in Bangalore, India in 1896. However, he did not find the exciting action he so desired. The British army was there only to maintain order and the soldiers spent most of their time relaxing and playing polo at night (Lyons, P. 3). While stationed here, Churchill realized the huge gaps in his education from his years at the Harrow School. "He sent home for more books and eagerly consumed classic works of history, philosophy, and politics. He read for four or five hours a day" (Lyons, P. 3). It seems that he wanted to catch up for what he had previously missed educationally in order to push himself forward academically, politically and socially. During his time in India, Churchill proved himself as a writer once again when an uprising broke out on the northwest frontier. Betting that the general in charge there would be able to make use of him, Churchill made the 2,500-mile journey to report about the uprising and sell his stories to an Indian newspaper and to the British Daily Telegraph. These stories were compiled in his first book, *The Story of the Malakand Field Force* (Lyons, P. 3). At this time, Churchill was also already dreaming of his futures successes. He frequently discussed his political ambitions with his fellow officers, saying, "'One day, I shall be Prime Minister'" (Lyons, P. 3). While at the time this seemed very unlikely, he was able to use his immense internal success drive to take him places no one thought he could go. Just as he once stated, "Success is stumbling from failure to failure without loss of enthusiasm".

After his adventures in India, Winston Churchill, then 25, headed to South Africa in 1899 to cover the Boer War, a war between British and Dutch settlers, as a newspaper correspondent for the *Morning Post*. However, his timing could not have been worse because he arrived just in time to be captured in an ambush carried out by Boer soldiers.. Luckily, he was able to escape from the prison in Pretoria after only a month of captivity. With only the clothes on his back, some chocolate, and a few hundred dollars, he was fortunate enough to stumble upon the home of some fellow British people who did not turn him in for the reward money When he finally made his way to a Britich controlled enclave in South Africa. (Churchill Center, 2007). This was the first time that Churchill was able to successfully use his cunning and creative abilities to survive and escape captivity. Upon being proclaimed a hero by the British forces,, he had the perfect opportunity to return to Britain and pursue the political career that he so desperately wanted.

Political Downfalls and Personal Struggles

Of everything that Winston Churchill ever undertook in his life, his political career is the one aspect for which he is remembered as being the most successful. In many people's eyes, he is a role model and a hero to look up to. However, it took many years before this was going to be the case. His political career began in 1900, when at the young, ripe age of 26 years old, Winston Churchill ran for parliament with all of the hopes and aspirations of any young politician. However, against all of his efforts, he lost his first election. This first political failure was just another obstacle for Churchill to overcome. The next year, he ran for parliament again and was successful. He became a Member of Parliament in the House of Commons as a member of of the Conservative Party (Keegan, P. 2). However, in 1904, Churchill left this party and joined the Liberals, something that many people negatively judged him for at the time.. However, unlike some of his decisions, he did have his a reason for this drastic switch in ideals. The Liberal Party was up and coming and he knew that this was the time to join, as he would be able to get a higher-ranking position. This paid off for young Winston for in 1910,he became Home Secretary and in 1911, he became First Lord of the Admiralty, or the political head of the Royal Navy (Keegan, P, 2). This was the time that Winston Churchill finally got the big break he deserved and became a real player on the world stage.

However, this success was unfortunately short lived. During WW1 In 1914 he led the Royal Navy in an attempt to block the German front and gain control of Dardanelles and Gallipoli Peninsula. These lands guarded the connection between the Black Sea and the Mediterranean. If this mission were successful, Britain could have aided Russia and prevented the terrible slaughter that was occurring in Western Europe. This mission ended up being a massive failure and haunted Churchill's political career for years to come (Keegan, P. 2). Responsible for over 46,000 deaths, he was eventually forced to resign from his position in the Royal Navy (Heffer, P. 5). This major failure illustrates how hard Churchill wanted to succeed and just how far he was willing to go to do it. "'He learned, he said, never to undertake a key operation of war without full authority to carry it out'" (Churchill Center, 2007). Due to his father's political failures, it is not surprising that Winston wanted to enter the world stage with a bang and become someone important immediately. However, it seems he tried too hard to succeed and this mistake became a major stain on his career and political fortunes.

In 1917, Churchill was reinstated into office as Minister of Munitions and then was War Secretary in 1919. Hungry for war, he again made the rash decision to attempt to intervene against the Bolshevik's in Russia. Thankfully, his colleagues vetoed his plan, which saved thousands of lives. By 1924, Churchill had switched back to the Conservative Party and was appointed

Chancellor of the Exchequer. This position put him in charge of Great Britain's finance and economics. However, Churchill had a huge lack of knowledge in this area and this resulted in another major failure in his political career (Keegan, P. 2). Disregarding the opinions of all economists he had access to, Churchill decided to move Britain, having just been ravaged by WWI, back to the gold standard at the pre-war fix price. This move devastated the economy even more and crippled all markets. He later said that this was the single greatest mistake of his life. Churchill, to his very core, was an idealist and true democrat. However, while these qualities came to save the world in the 1940's, they nearly ruined Britain a few decades earlier.

After resigning from his office as Chancellor of the Exchequer in 1931, Churchill entered into a period of political decline. During this time he flourished as a writer and journalist. It was crucial that he had these skills as his financial situation had become difficult and he needed the money from those activites to support his life style. . He was also having marital issues as his wife, Clementine Churchill, was feeling neglected and also did not like his circle of friends. At this time, there were also rumors that Churchill's son, Randolph, was illegitimate. This made their relationship difficult, as Randolph was never able to emerge from under his father's shadow and became an alcoholic at an early age (Heffer, P. 6).

In these pre-war years, Churchill knew he had to take a strong stance against Hitler in order to be the one man that the nation could turn to when the confrontation between Britain and Hitler finally arrived in 1940 (Keegan, P. 3). Churchil stood as a stark contrast to Neville Chamberlain, who eventually lost the trust of parliament. When this happened, Churchill became

Prime Minister, a job he had been seeking for over 40 years. This was finally the chance at success that he had been dreaming of his entire life. Despite his prior failures, he was now the most powerful man in Britain.

WWII Successes and Post-War Life

Thankfully, Winston Churchill was a smart man who had learned from the mistakes he made during WWI. This time around, while he still took many bold initiatives, most of them paid off in substantial ways. His ability to compromise with Stalin for the good of Britain demonstrates his clear thinking , moral strength and level-headedness during times of extreme pressure. His decisive plan to oppose Hitler by stopping Mussolini and then creating an alliance with Russia and the United States is another example of this. It is hard to think of anyone else who "would have led Britain with such certainty of moral purpose and inspiration and who had the qualities to handle our allies so well" (Heffer, P. 7). His successes in WWII not only saved Britain from the evil of Naziism, but the world as well. His triumph over Hitler earned him a lifetime of deference. He stands, totally unchallenged, as the greatest of all of Britain's wartime leaders (Keegan, P. 4). It could be argued that his victory over Hitler, was a victory of moral integrity over the forces of great evil.

In 1945, the Labor party defeated the Conservatives in parliament and Churchill was no longer Prime Minister. However by 1951, the Conservatives had regained their power and Churchill was again the Prime Minister. At this time, the biggest threat was that of nuclear war between the United Stated and the Soviet Union. Churchill gave riveting speeches warning of the Iron Curtain in Europe (Churchill Center, 2007).

Churchill maintained his position of leadership until 1955 when he was 81 years old, despite suffering a debilitating stroke two years earlier,, and still remained as a Member of Parliament for nine more years (Churchill Center, 2007).

Despite his many misjudgments and failures, Winston Churchill is one the greatest politicians and wartime heroes that has ever lived. His indisputable greatness, however, has come in spite of, not because of, his imperfect characteristics. The important thing to remember, though, is that no matter how often or how hard he failed, he always picked himself back up and strived for greatness and moral integrity This fact begs the question, however, as to what allowed to him to do this? Was it an attempt to prove his family wrong? Did he just get lucky or did he have a tremendously strong S-Factor that became the foundation and engine of his success. The following represents my analysis of how the six sub-elements of Taccarino's theory of the S-Factor contributed to Churchill's success.

Internal Motivation and Self-Regulation

Winston Churchill had this amazing characteristic and it was demonstrated in the way that he declared that he would be Prime Minister when he was only 22 years old. He was able to achieve this life goal strictly though motivating himself. He had no one standing in his corner; in fact, most people were against him for a majority of his life. After repeated political failures, he never gave up. Being able to achieve something so great on his own accord shows just the type of self-regulating characteristics that Churchill had. It was these characteristics, such as persistence and resilience, that allowed him to achieve his lifelong dream.

Self-Valuing

If Winston Churchill did not achieve self-valuing, he would have given up after his many failures. He did not fail as a political and military leaader once, but many times. The fact that he could brush these failures off and continue to be resolute in his dreams shows his immense self-valuing and just how much he believed in himself and the moral worthiness of his efforts.

Affective Effectiveness

Winston Churchill was able to use to use his affective effectiveness to solve many difficult and complicated problems in his life and also to motivate and convince others that his plan to defeat Hitler was the best option. While Churchill had many personal struggles to overcome, like his relationship with his father, he never let his emotions get the best of him and continued to strive towards his goal no matter what. Even in the face of the biggest public embarrassments of his life, he remained calm under pressure and was resilient. Much of this was grounded in the strength of his integrity and moral commitments.

Interpersonal Effectiveness

This element of the S-Factor was epitomized in Winston Churchill's ability to convince a nation to let him lead them out of the darkness of war and the threat of Naziism. It was in many ways his moral opposition to to Naziism that gave strength to his nation in the dark days of the bombing of London. Even with a past riddled with failure and public humiliation, he was able to persuade others to place their trust in him. Through his strong interpersonal effectiveness and moral strength , Churchill was able to transform himself from a political failure to a national hero within a few short years.

Self-Potency

"People with high levels of self-potency could be described as "larger than life", which is definitely something that was clearly descriptive of Winston Churchill after he left Sandhurst with a diploma and a transformed S-Factor. He had clearly how to succeed by seeking and acting upon his opportunities. While living in one of the darkest periods of recent history, life could not have been easy for Churchill. However, he romanticized about Britain's glory days and always strived to return it to its former greatness. He was incredibly ambitious and was always striving to do and be more.

Success Drive

It would be hard to argue that Winston Churchill was not dealt a great hand in the deck of life. He came from an affluent family, one with prominence and stature in British society. He had everything he could have ever dreamed of as a child and received the best education. However, all of these things add up to nothing if he did not develop a strong success drive in a personal transformation from the aimlessness of his childhood. . Individuals with a strong success drive are "ambitious, self-motivated, resilient and have a strong need to succeed" (Taccarino, P. 6). After failing countless times in life, academically and politically, Churchill never gave up and continued to strive towards his lifelong dream of becoming Prime Minister. On top of this, he also helped win the greatest war in history and saved his nation and the world from the dark shadow of a Nazi future.

Conclusions

Churchill was not a perfect man as he did make moral mistakes that he regretted such as the betrayal of Poland in the Yalta Agreements with Stalin. When thirty Polish aviators who had fought with British forces against Germany committed suicide after the Allies allowed Russia to take over Poland, Churchill's moral substance caused him to have a crisis of conscience that drove him to seek the freedom of Poland in the post-war era. Churchill was not a morally perfect man, but he was a man of conscience who used the strength of his S-Factor to seek to right moral wrongs, even those of his own making.

Both Hitler and Churchill overcame patterns of under-achievement in their youths and developed strong S-Factors in their adult years. Both Hitler and Churchill had learned how to succeed, but Churchill also learned that lasting success has to be built upon a foundation of ethics and morality. This is obviously a lesson that Hitler had never learned.

REFERENCES

Heffer, Simon. "The Churchill Myth." *New Statesman* (2015): 18-23. Web. 2016.

Keegan, John. "Winston Churchill." *Time* 151.14 (1998): 114. Web. 2016.

Lyons, Justin D. "Young Churchill: Adventure with Purpose." *Dig Into History* 17.5 (2015): 8-10. Web. 2016.

Taccarino, John. *Success Readiness Development.* Retrieved from, https://d2l.depaul.edu/d2l/le/content/349634/viewContent/2511972/View

"The Life of Winston Churchill." *The Churchill Center.* 2007. Web. 2016.

APPENDIX A

A REVIEW OF THE GENERAL RESEARCH LITERATURE PERTAINING TO THE TACCARINO-LEONARD S (SUCCESS)-FACTOR

By John Taccarino

This chapter is drawn from the book "S(Success)-Factor, the Psychological Roots of Success" (Taccarino et al, 2015) provides an overview of research that supports both the existence and effectiveness of the S-Factor as an engine and an indicator of academic achievement and career success.

A doctoral study (Chipain, 2003) established an important link between S-Factor strength and sales performance. In Chipain's study, the Success Tendencies Indicator (an earlier form of the **TLSFP**) was administered to a sample of 128 persons who were employed as sales professionals by a home products firm in the Chicago area. A correlation coefficient of .42 was found between the subjects' scores on Success Tendencies

Indicator and their sales generated income levels. When looking at the top quartile of salespersons with respect to their income levels, Chipain found a correlation coefficient of .63 between their income levels and scores on the Success Tendencies Scale. When assessing the bottom quartile of salespersons with respect to their income levels, he found a correlation coefficient of .57 between their income levels and their scores on the Success Tendencies Scale. Strongly supporting the construct of the relative strength of the S-Factor as an indicator of career success, a t-test analysis of the mean Success Tendencies Scale scores of those in the top quartile in income and the mean scores of those in the bottom quartile income yielded a t-value that was statistically significant at the .001 level.

In another study (Taccarino and Leonard, 1998) to assess the construct of the S-Factor as an indicator of social effectiveness, the Success Tendencies Scale (a measure of overall s-Factor strength) was administered to a sample of graduate students (N=64) at DePaul University who were also administered the California Psychological Inventory, an assessment measuring the dimensions of social personality. Statistically significant correlations (Pearson Product Moment Method) were found between the S-Factor, as measured by the Success Tendencies Scale, and the following scales of the California Psychological Inventory: Dominance (.42), Leadership potential (.42), Sociability (.47), Capacity for Status (.39), Independence (.33), Self-acceptance (.35), and Social Maturity (.32). These findings suggest that the S-Factor, as measured by the Success Tendencies Scale, is assessing a construct of social and affective effectiveness that has some similarity to a cluster of scales found within the California Psychological Inventory.

Bartlett (1998) employed the Achievement Tendencies Scale (now re-titled the Success Tendencies Scale) as a measure of emotional intelligence in a study conducted at Stevenson High School in Lincolnshire, Illinois. Stevenson High School has twice received the United States Department of Education's Excellence in Education Award and has been listed by Redbook Magazine as one of the best academic high schools in America.

The study was motivated by Goleman's (1995) contention that emotional intelligence is a better predictor of life success than either I.Q. (Intelligence Quotient) or Scholastic Aptitude Test (SAT) scores. In assessing the content and construct validity of the Achievement Tendencies Scale as a measure of emotional intelligence, Bartlett compared the items contained within the Achievement Tendencies Scale with the A Self Science Curriculum developed by Stone and Dillehunt (1978). This curriculum was described by Goleman as a model course in emotional intelligence (1995, p. 261) and an almost point-for- point match with the ingredients of emotional intelligence. Bartlett found in his analysis that with a liberal interpretation, the Achievement Tendencies Scale can be considered to include items in 13 of 13 categories of Self Science: self awareness (32), personal decision making (22), managing feelings (10), handling stress (4), empathy (5), communications (17), self disclosure (35), insight (34), self acceptance (7), personal responsibility (16), assertiveness (7), group dynamics (20), and conflict resolution (13) (Bartlett, 1998, p.96). As a predictor of emotional intelligence, Bartlett sought to assess whether the Achievement Tendencies Scale could distinguish high and low academic achievement groups, as determined by grade point averages, and high and low behavioral adjustment groups, as determined by frequency of referrals to the Dean's office for behavior problems. Employing a sample of eighty male and female sophomores at Stevenson High School, the study reported higher mean Achievement Tendencies Scale (presently titled the Success Tendencies Scale) scores for males, females, and males and females combined for the high academic achievement groups than the low academic achievement groups. The differences between the mean scores of the criterion groups were statistically significant at the .01 probability level (Bartlett, 1998, p.114).

The study also found that males and females in the low behavior problem group, as measured by frequency of Dean's Office referral's, had a higher mean Achievement Tendencies Scale score than the mean score for the group who had a high frequency of Dean's Office referral's. The difference between the means was statistically significant at the .05 probability level (Bartlett, 1998, p. 129).

In his study Bartlett used The Achievement Tendencies Scale. Although emotional intelligence can be subsumed within the construct of the S-Factor (its sub-factor elements such as affective effectiveness, internal motivation and interpersonal effectiveness are key components of emotional intelligence), it is the author's belief that the Success Tendencies Scale is measuring a broader construct than emotional intelligence alone. As a result, if the Success Tendencies Scale is measuring the S-Factor then the findings of the study can support the effectiveness of the S-Factor as an indicator of emotional intelligence, academic achievement and behavioral adjustment as it applies to this particular study.

In a subsequent doctoral study conducted at Rolling Meadows High School in Rolling Meadows Illinois, Bartlett

(2003) evaluated the effectiveness of S-Factor assessment as an indicator of academic achievement. Using the Success Tendencies Indicator as a measure of the S-Factor, Bartlett in a study of 338 students found a statistically significant correlation of .49 between the students' grade point averages and scores on the Success Tendencies Scale. Further, a correlation of .68 was found between the students' grade point averages and their scores on the Success Tendencies Indicator's Internal Motivation and Self Regulation Sub-scale (a measure of an interrelated sub-element of the S-Factor). A correlation at this level provides very strong evidence that the relative strength of a student's S-factor is a powerful indicator of academic performance. It also raises the possibility that the Internal Motivation and Self –Regulation Sub-scale could be used in conjunction with ACT or SAT scores to improve the validity of college admissions screening. Additionally, Bartlett found a .40 correlation between reported disciplinary incidents and scores on the Internal Motivation and Self-Regulation Sub-scale. This finding suggests that students who score higher on the Internal Motivation and Self Regulation Sub-scale are less likely to be involved in disciplinary incidents than those with lower scores. It also provides support for the S-Factor as an indicator of impulse control and self-regulation.

The ability of the Success Tendencies Scale to distinguish between those who achieve leadership positions in high school and those who do not was assessed in a study (Taccarino and Leonard, 1998) in which 338 Chicago area high school students, undergraduate students and graduate students were administered the Success Tendencies Scale. Statistically significant differences were found at the .001 probability level between the mean Success Tendencies Scale score for individuals who held office in student government in high school or college and the mean score of those who did not. Because the mean Success Tendencies Scale score was higher at a statistically significant level for those who held a leadership position in student government, the finding supported the effectiveness of S-Factor assessment as an indicator of those who will achieve leadership positions.

In a further study (Taccarino and Leonard, 1998) of Chicago area adults, the mean Success Tendencies Scale score of 48 individuals who did not go to college were compared with the mean score of 114 individuals who were attending or had attended college. The significantly higher (.001 probability level) mean score for the group who were attending or had attended college supported the effectiveness of S-Factor assessment as a predictor of academic attainment levels.

Also, the same study found a statistically significant (001 probability) higher Success Tendencies Scale mean score for students who attended graduate or professional school than the mean for those who attended college, but did not go beyond the undergraduate level. This further supports the effectiveness of S-Factor assessment in discriminating academic attainment levels even within a relatively high achieving population.

Another study (Taccarino and Leonard, 1998) was conducted to assess the effectiveness of the Success Tendencies Scale in distinguishing college educated adults in Illinois who could be identified as high achievers as measured by career success from those identified as average or low achievers as measured by career success. Graduate students within the DePaul University School of Education administered the Success Tendencies Scale to a sample of 34 college-educated adults identified as high achievers and 29 college educated adults identified as average and low achievers. A t-test analysis indicated that a statistically significant (.01 probability level) difference was found between the higher mean Success Tendencies Scale score (44.82) for the sample identified as high achievers than the mean score (35.62) for the sample of average and low achievers.

This finding tends to support the effectiveness of S-Factor assessment in identifying levels of achievement attainment and career success. It also provides evidence of the construct validity of the Success Tendencies Scale as a measure of the S-Factor. To support the construct validity of this assessment those identified as high achievers should score in ranges that suggest strong success tendencies. Consistent with that expectancy, the mean Success Tendencies Scale score for the group identified as high achievers was 44.82. According to the interpretation criteria for the Success Tendencies Scale, a mean score of 44.82 would be in the Strong S-Factor range. According to the interpretation guidelines cited on page 6 of the Manual for the Success Tendencies Indicator, (Taccarino and Leonard, 1998), Students scoring in this range generally exhibit the tendency to be motivated, self- directed achievers who could perform well in most settings.

Royster (2004) conducted case study analyses of five high achieving African American males who were identified by Taccarino-Leonard's Suceess Tendencies scale as exhibiting strong S-Factors. Her findings indicated that a strong S-Factor has an important underlying influence on the variables that supported the achievement patterns of the successful African American males who were the subjects for her case studies. The details of this study are further presented in Chapter 7.

A pilot study (2015) was conducted by the MirrorWalk Corporation in Hong Kong to assess the validity of S-Factor assessments when applied to a Chinese population of primary and middle school students. In the study S-Factor assessments were administered to four hundred students attending seven schools located in Beijing and Shanghai. In the study Ms. Leslie Wang (CEO of MirrorWalk) supervised the administrations and collections of the data drawn from the administration of the S-Factor assessments. Mr. Nimod Athiyarath conducted the statistical analyses of the data and Dr. John Taccarino interpreted the data.

Regarding the results of the study, a high Pearson Product Moment correlation coefficient (.71) was found between the students overall S-Factor scores and their scores on the Introversion/ Extroversion scale. This supports the expected finding that introverts will manifest stronger S-Factors than extroverts. The high correlation coefficient (77) found between the students overall S-Factor scores and their scores on the Analytical/ Creativity Scale supports the expected finding that students with Analytical Personality types will have stronger S-Factors than those with Creative Personality types. This finding that introverted and analytical personality types are associated with S-Factor strength suggests that the assessment is exhibiting construct validity in that the expected correlations are being manifested in the collected sample of Chinese Students. A body of research has indicated that students with introverted, analytical personality types perform at a higher level academically than students who are creative and extroverted. This supports the validity of S-Factor assessment as it applies to a Chinese sample.

Another key finding of this study indicated very high Pearson Product Moment correlations between the students' overall S-Factor scores and their scores on the sub-elements of the S-Factor assessments.: Internal Motivation and Self-Regulation, .91 correlation coefficient, Success Drive .98 correlation coefficient, Self valuing, .93 correlation coefficient, Affective Effectiveness, .92 correlation coefficient, Interpersonal Effectiveness, .90 correlation coefficient , and Self-Potency, .97 correlation coefficient. These findings are important because they supports the validity of the core concept of the 'S-Factor that self-valuing, internal motivation and self-regulation, affective effectiveness, interpersonal effectiveness, self potency and success drive are internally consistent and interrelated sub-elements of the 'S-Factor for this sample of Chinese students. These findings are also a significant basis for establishing that the operations of S-Factor assessment for Chinese students function in the same manner as it does in prior validity studies applied to samples of American students.

In conclusion, the emerging body of research that has been cited suggests support for the existence of the S-Factor and its potential effectiveness as an indicator of academic achievement, career success and personal effectiveness. Further independent research upon the S-Factor and its correlates is obviously greatly encouraged.

REFERENCES

Bartlett, T.L. (1998). *The Relationship Between Student Emotional Intelligence and Academic Achievement and Behavioral Adjustment.* M.A. Thesis. Chicago: DePaul University

Bartlett, T.L. (2003) *The Relationship Between the Success Tendencies Indicator and Academic Achievement and Behavioral Adjustment.* Doctoral Research in Progress, Chicago: DePaul University

Chipain, George (2003). *The Relationship Between Emotional Intelligence and Sales Success.* Doctoral Dissertation. Chicago: DePaul University

Goleman, D. (1995). *Emotional Intelligence.* New York: Bantam Books

Leonard, M. and J. Taccarino (1998). *Manual for the Success Tendencies Indicator. Revised.* Chicago: John Taccarino and Associates

Leonard, M. and J. Taccarino (1998). *The Success Tendencies Indicator, Assessment Booklet.* John Taccarino and Associates

Leonard, M. and J. Taccarino (2003). *The Success Tendencies Indicator: High School and College Form.* Chicago: Seastar Communications

Leonard, M. and J. Taccarino (2003). *Manual for the Success Tendencies Indicator: High School and College Form: Assessment Booklet.* Chicago: Seastar Communications

Leonard, M. and J. Taccarino (2003). *Manual for the Success Tendencies Indicator for Children.* Chicago: Seastar Communications

Leonard, M. and J. Taccarino (2003). *The Success Tendencies Indicator for Children: Assessment Booklet*. Chicago: Seastar Communications

Royster, S. (2004), *Success Tendencies Indicators for African American Men*, M.A. Thesis: Chicago: DePaul University

Stone, H.K. and H.Q. Dilehunt (1978). *Self Science: The Subject is Me*. Santa Monica, California: Goodyear Publishing Co.

CPSIA information can be obtained
at www.ICGtesting.com
Printed in the USA
LVHW04s0404250418
574741LV00001B/1/P